Physical Characteristics of
the Cavalier King Charles Spaniel
(from the American Kennel Club breed standard)

Body: Short-coupled with ribs well spring.

Hindquarters: Moderately muscled; pelvis broad, stifles well turned and hocks well let down.

Coat: Of moderate length, silky, free from curl. Slight wave permissible. Feathering on ears, chest, legs and tail should be long. and the feathering on the feet is a feature of the breed.

Color: Blenheim - Rich chestnut markings well broken up on a clear, pearly white ground. The ears must be chestnut and the color evenly spaced on the head and surrounding both eyes, with a white blaze between the eyes and ears, in the center of which may be the lozenge or "Blenheim spot." Other colors are Tricolor, Ruby and Black and Tan.

Tail: Well set on, carried happily but never much above the level of the back.

Size: Height 12 to 13 inches at the withers; weight proportionate to height, between 13 and 18 pounds.

Cavalier King Charles Spaniel

◇

by Juliette Cunliffe

Contents

KENNEL CLUB BOOKS® CAVALIER KING CHARLES SPANIEL
ISBN: 1-59378-214-4

Copyright © 2004, 2005 • Kennel Club Books, LLC
308 Main Street, Allenhurst, NJ 07711 USA
Cover Design Patented: US 6,435,559 B2 • Printed in South Korea

Photographs by Carol Ann Johnson
Additional photos provided by: Norvia Behling, Carolina Biological Supply, David Dalton Doskocil, Isabelle Francais, James Hayden-Yoav, James R. Hayden, REP, Dwight R. Kuhn, Dr. Dennis Kunkel, Mikki Pet Products, Phototake, Jean Claude Revy, Dr. Andrew Spielman, Karen Taylor, C. James Webb.

Illustrations by Renée Low.

HISTORY OF THE

CAVALIER KING CHARLES SPANIEL

The charming Cavalier King Charles Spaniel can trace his ancestors back to the small toy spaniels that are found in many paintings of the 16th, 17th and 18th centuries. Such dogs were favorites of royalty and nobles of the day and because of this many were depicted with their owners and with children, making for some delightful family groups. The first portrait in England that depicts the breed is one of Queen Mary I with her husband, Philip of Spain, accompanied by a pair of small spaniels lying at their feet. It was painted in 1554 by Antonio Moro. Well-respected artists such as Titian, Van Dyck, Stubbs, Gainsborough and Reynolds all showed similar small dogs with flat heads, high-set ears and slightly pointed noses.

The devotion of the Cavalier is legendary as it was a little black and white toy spaniel that hid beneath the skirts of Mary Queen of Scots at her execution in 1587. Even after her death, it would not leave its dead mistress for it was recorded, "Then one of the executioners, pulling off her garters, espied her little dogg which was crept under her clothes which could not be gotten forth but by force, yet afterwards would not depart from the dead corpse, but came and lay between her head and her shoulders..."

During Tudor times (1485–1603) these small spaniels were highly popular as ladies' pets and under the House of Stuart (1603–1714) they were actually given the name King Charles Spaniels. King Charles I was

accompanied by a small spaniel when he was a fugitive at Carisbrook Castle. After he had been executed, his dog, Rogue, was paraded around the city by a Roundhead, though the fate of the little dog is not known. But it was really thanks to King Charles II that the breed took its name.

A great lover of these dogs, Charles II was almost always seen with some of his small canine friends at his heels. The famous diarist Samuel Pepys made many references to them, showing dismay that the King played all the while with his dogs rather than minding business affairs. The King even decreed that these spaniels were to be allowed in any public place, including the Houses of Parliament.

James II was another king reputed to be fond of the breed, and there is record of him giving orders during a bad sea storm that the men were to "save the dogs! … and the Duke of Monmouth!" One

SPANISH ORIGINS

Some people believe that all spaniels originated in Spain and that they actually took their name from the word "espagñol," which means Spanish. It is also believed that the black Truffle Dog may lie behind black and tan colored Cavaliers.

can only wonder if there was any significance in his mentioning the dogs before the Duke!

Undoubtedly spaniels of this kind were much in favor in many of the European courts, but although the red and white variety bred at Blenheim Palace retained its popularity, the others seemed to go somewhat out of fashion. This was thanks largely to the accession to the throne of William and Mary, who highly favored Pugs.

The merry toy spaniels that had scampered about the palaces and had appeared on numerous state occasions were, it might be said, demoted by the House of Orange. The Pugs smugly took their place. Some believe that it was because of the newfound popularity of the Pug that some enthusiasts of King Charles Spaniels decided that a certain change in the breed's features would perhaps be an improvement.

During the early years of the 19th century, the small spaniel once again rose in the popularity stakes for the Duke of Marlborough used small spaniels as shooting companions. These were a little larger than the Cavaliers known today. In 1820 his dogs were described as "very small or carpet spaniels." They were red and white, with very long ears, short noses and black eyes. Still today, what is known as the lozenge spot on the head of some Cavalier King Charles Spaniels is highly prized, and there is a delightful story as to how this came about. The Duchess of Marlborough had one of these spaniels as a much-loved pet which kept her company while her husband was away at war. At anxious times she had the habit of pressing her thumb on her dog's head while awaiting news of her husband. When the bitch produced a litter of puppies the head of each was marked with her thumbprint.

Once known as Gredin, the black Cavalier of yesterday much resembles the variety we know as Black and Tan.

Hitherto these spaniels had been brown and white, black and white or tricolor. In the past there were black spaniels but they were known as Gredin, although they were very much like today's black and tans, with tan eyebrows, muzzles, throats and legs, known as "fire-marks." It was not until the reign of Queen Victoria that ruby-colored spaniels appeared. In her youth, Queen Victoria owned a small spaniel called Dash, a tricolor. So fond was she of Dash that after her Coronation in 1838 she was said to have rushed home to give her dog his usual bath. Dash was a familiar little figure and appeared on many pieces of needlework sewn by Victorian women. The first known painting of a ruby is one in which the Duke and Duchess of Cumberland were pictured walking with such a dog. A gentleman by the name of Mr. Risum is reputed to have owned the first known ruby and this won second prize at the Alexandra Palace Show in 1875.

Undoubtedly in the early years both size and type varied within the breed, so it may be surmised

The ever-popular red and white Cavalier, called the Blenheim, received its name from the Blenheim Palace where the dogs were bred.

MALTESE FOUNDER
Although the true origin of today's Cavalier is not really known, the breed may originally have developed from a red and white spaniel of Malta or Italy, this having been crossed in the 13th century with a type of spaniel from the Far East.

that at that time breeding was carried out in something of a haphazard way. However, as the 19th century moved on in Britain, dog showing was starting to become a popular pastime and the breed saw a new fashion emerge. Soon enough the so-called "old type" had begun to disappear: the longer nosed, flat-headed dogs having been replaced by a much shorter faced, dome-headed dog now known as the King Charles Spaniel. In the US, the breed became known as the English Toy Spaniel. It was believed that the Pug may have been used in breeding programs in order to help bring about this significant change. In 1886 the Toy Spaniel Club was founded, but in 1902 the organization changed its name to the King Charles Spaniel Club, even though initially the English Kennel Club was opposed to this change of name. Once again royal interest worked in favor of the breed and Edward VII intervened, subsequent to which the new name was approved.

The First World War had a disastrous effect on King Charles Spaniels, as indeed it did on so many breeds of dog. An American gentleman by the name of Roswell Eldridge had been to Britain to search for a pair of these dogs and dearly wanted to re-kindle interest in the breed.

In the Crufts show schedule for 1926, King Charles Spaniel enthusiasts were startled by an announcement that this same Mr. Roswell Eldridge of New York was offering two prizes of £25 each for "Blenheim spaniels of the old type as shown in Charles II's time: long face, no stop, flat skull not inclined to be domed, with spot in centre of skull." This was a far cry from the King Charles being shown at that time. Interestingly the suggested models to comply with this stipulation were those shown in Landseer's painting, despite the fact that these did have a slight indentation between the eyes, known as a stop. Although this was shallow, the request for no stop was probably rather confusing for exhibitors, especially those who had already spent many years actually developing a more "squashed-in" nose, with a more accentuated stop and a domed skull.

To begin with, there were few competitors for the special prizes on offer, but a handful of breeders decided to re-develop the toy spaniels according to Mr. Eldridge's description. Two years later, in 1928, a special club was formed for this particular type, although there were then still very few of them. The selection of a name caused much heart-searching for breeders did not want to lose the name "King Charles." Eventually the name "Cavalier King Charles Spaniel" was selected. A standard of points was drawn up for the breed, using Ann's Son, an early winner of Mr. Eldridge's prize, as the dog on which the standard was based. In fact it is Ann's Son and five other dogs that formed the foundation of the Cavalier King Charles Spaniel we know today.

However, things could not progress as quickly as may have been wished. There were still only few dogs in number and the English Kennel Club was not prepared to grant the breed separate status, indeed not for the next 17 years! Meanwhile these dogs were known as King Charles Spaniels (old type) and were shown in the same classes as the King Charles.

In 1945 the English Kennel Club thought it right to grant separate classification to the Cavalier King Charles Spaniel and to grant

A tricolored Cavalier, the variety preferred by Queen Victoria, is black and tan with a white ground color.

the breed championship status. Sadly Mr. Roswell Eldridge had died long before, in 1928, so he did not have the fulfillment of knowing that the dogs he so loved had gained official recognition. The first Championship Show for the breed was held at Stratford-upon-Avon on August 29, 1946, when Best in Show was awarded to Mrs. Eldred's Belinda of Saxham, a Blenheim. The first Cavalier to gain his Championship

FAMOUS FANCIERS

Among many well-known people who have owned Cavalier King Charles Spaniels in recent years are Her Royal Highness Princess Margaret, Nigel Lawsor and former President Ronald and First Lady Nancy Reagan.

title, this in 1948, was Daywell Roger, who had been awarded Best Dog at the first Championship Show. He was a successful sire with several champion offspring who were to have great influence on the breed in the years ahead.

The breed quickly gained popularity in Britain and among the toy breeds was only surpassed in popularity by what were then described as the "rave breeds," Yorkshire Terrier, Pekingese and Smooth Coated Chihuahuas. In Britain between the years 1954 and 1964, the number of Kennel Club annual registrations for the breed had risen from 794 to 2,352, by which time registrations for the King Charles Spaniel amounted only to 170. By 1966 the Cavalier climbed into The Kennel Club's "Top Twenty" list of breeds. This was undoubtedly in part because the breed was by then winning well at shows. In 1963 Amelia of

The Cavalier King Charles Spaniel was recognized as a separate breed by the English Kennel Club in 1945. In no time at all, it became the most popular toy dog in Britain.

Laguna had won Best Toy at Crufts and then Best Bitch of all breeds on the first day of the show, while in New Zealand a Cavalier by the name of Sugar Crisp of Ttiweh had won Best in Show all breeds at a Championship Show. There was no turning back now.

As the 1960s drew to their close, Britain's Cavalier King Charles Spaniel Club had over 400 members, comprising a keen and lively body of people, helped and encouraged by its officers and committee. Many Cavaliers have won high accolades at shows and in 1973 Alansmere Aquarius, owned by Messrs. Hall and Evans, won what is perhaps the most famous award of all, Best in Show at Crufts.

THE BREED AROUND THE WORLD

In Europe the Cavalier King Charles Spaniel is shown under the rules of the Fédération Cynologique Internationale (FCI) in Group 9 and in Section 7, which is for English Toy Spaniels, the other breed in this group being the King Charles. The Cavalier is also divided by color into: a) Black and tan, b) Ruby, c) Blenheim and d) Tricolor. The number of entries at European shows varies considerably according to the country and the prestige of the show, ease of accessibility and so on. The World Dog Show moves from country to country

and can attract approaching 100 Cavaliers, whereas at Crufts there may be as many as 400 or more.

In mainland Europe, Cavaliers had become fairly popular in Holland during the breed's relatively early days, and certain interest in the breed has grown in Germany and in Italy. In Sweden the Cavalier went from strength to strength with registrations rising rapidly through the 1960s and 1970s, and now the breed has captivated the hearts of numerous dedicated breeders in many countries throughout the world.

In Canada the breed gained recognition in 1957, and by 1964 a small number of Cavaliers were being shown. The following year, 1965, saw the breed's first Canadian Champion, Pargeter Flashback. Since then the breed has grown enormously in popularity, and in recent years has often found itself with the largest entry in the Toy Group at shows.

The breed did not arrive in Australia until 1960 where the Cavalier's early history centered primarily around dogs in Victoria,

Cavaliers are popular as show dogs and pets around the world.

New South Wales and Western Australia. The Blenheim bitch, Soylanc Begonia, imported in whelp from New Zealand, was to become the country's first champion. Numbers grew steadily from then on especially during the 1970s, and in 1978 Lady Forward, Patron of the New South Wales Club, was invited to judge the tenth anniversary show, beginning a tradition of continued co-operation with Cavalier breed enthusiasts throughout the world.

THE CAVALIER IN THE US

The English Toy Spaniel (known in the Mother country as the King Charles Spaniel) had been established in the US since the early 20th century, when the first dogs were registered in 1902. The breed was divided into separate classifications for solids and parti-colors, which means that there are two English Toy Spaniels in the Group competition at all AKC shows.

The Cavalier King Charles Spaniel is a more recent phenomenon in the US, and when Lady

The King Charles Spaniel, also known as the English Toy Spaniel, has fallen in popularity, while the Cavalier has topped the list of most popular toy dogs.

Mary Forwood sent a black and tan pup here from England in 1952, there were only five Cavaliers in the whole country! The first Cavalier to enter the US, it is believed, did so in 1946, a male, Robrull of Veren, owned by Mrs. Harold Whitman of New York. The second arrived the following year, Bertie of Rookerynook, also a male, to Mrs. John Schiff, also of New York. These two pioneer Cavaliers, however, did not have the impact that Lady Forwood's gift would have. Mrs. W. L. Lyons Brown (Sally) received Lady Forwood's gift, Psyche of Eyeworth, to her home in Kentucky. Sally Brown became the president of the Cavalier King Charles Spaniel Club, United States of America (CKCSC, USA), which was founded in 1954 as the breed's registering body.

The first national specialty took place in 1962, when the club had 72 members and 76 Cavaliers registered. There were 41 entries by 26 fanciers and 35 dogs. Elizabeth Spalding of Maine won with her Pargeter Lotus of Kilspindie (Best of Breed) and her Pargeter Mermaid (Best of Opposite). Another fancier who had tremendous impact on the Cavalier in the US was Gertrude Polk Brown Albrecht, the tireless patroness of the breed, the first registrar of the breed and the club's second president in 1962, a post she held for many years. She was followed upon her death, in 1983, by Elizabeth Spalding, who long had been active in the breed. Although the CKCSC, USA did not join the American Kennel Club, the breed entered the Miscellaneous Class in April 1962.

Cavaliers competed in the Miscellaneous Class from the 1960s to the late 1990s, though never in great numbers due to the member's negative feelings about the registry. The club's shows were well attended, and the breed had become quite popular in the US, as it had in every country around the world. The US was the only country where the breed was not accepted by the country's major all-breed registry, the AKC. Most members of the CKCSC, USA strongly opposed the breed's joining the AKC and club representatives told AKC representatives so at a meeting in 1993. The AKC, nonetheless, was firmly committed to accepting the breed, which had "parked" in the Miscellaneous Class for nearly 30 years. A vote in 1994 had 90% of the members voting against AKC membership, despite the AKC's well-known position.

As a result, a second breed club was formed to be the Cavalier's AKC parent club. The new club is called the American Cavalier King Charles Spaniel Club, and it was founded in 1994 by a group of 150 dedicated Cavalier fanciers, most of whom were long-time breeders and members of the CKCSC, USA. The AKC accepted the new club as the parent club, and the breed was recognized on January 1, 1996, becoming the AKC's 140th recognized breed. The new club's first specialty was held in 1997. The CKCSC, USA operates today as an independent registry for the breed, holding its own specialty shows and offering its own championship titles.

At the 1997 Westminster Kennel Club Show, the Cavalier's first appearance at this famous show, Ch. Partridge Wood

Laughing Misdemeanor, a six-year-old Ruby bitch, bred by Debra King and owner-handled by Cindy Lazzeroni, became the first Best of Breed as well as Group 4 in the show. The Best of Opposite Sex was Ch. Ravenrush Gillespie, owned by John D. Gammon and Robert A. Schroll. Among the breeders who have made an impact on the breed in the US are Joan Twigg, Robert and Barbara Garnett Smith, John D. Gammon, Robert A. Schroll, Robbi Jones, J. Anne Thaeder, Albert and Meredith Snyder, Paul Camponozzi, Cynthia Roof, Ted and Mary Grace Eubank, Brigida Reynolds, Janet York Piccadil, Martha Guimond, J. G.A. Boelaars, Harold and Joan Letterly and Olive Darbyshire.

After much ado and "adon't," the Cavalier finally became the AKC's 140th recognized breed.

CHARACTERISTICS OF THE
CAVALIER KING CHARLES SPANIEL

There are many excellent reasons why one should select the Cavalier King Charles Spaniel as a pet, or even as a show dog. This is an affectionate, playful, intelligent, small dog that is only too willing to repay an owner's care and attention with complete devotion.

Although undoubtedly considered a lap dog because of his size, the Cavalier is an absolutely fearless, sporting little dog. He is gay, friendly and non-aggressive and makes an excellent and adaptable companion for many different homes and lifestyles.

PHYSICAL CHARACTERISTICS
This is undisputedly a small breed, but one that is neither too small nor too delicate. The largest of the breeds within the Toy Group, the Cavalier is considerably larger than his cousin, the King Charles Spaniel that weighs on average about 4 pounds. Cavaliers do vary quite considerably in size, but, on the average, should weigh between 12–18 pounds.

The disparity in size between the different Cavaliers one comes across can easily confuse those not familiar with the breed. The bone is fairly heavy and so a small dog can weigh perhaps more than one could expect at first glance. On the other hand, a taller, more lightly boned Cavalier may actually weigh less than a smaller representative of the breed. However, this is a Toy breed and should in no way compare, for example, to a small Springer Spaniel.

It is within most people's capacity to pick up and carry the Cavalier when necessary, and at shows this breed is lifted onto a table for assessment by the judge. Because it such a charming breed, it is often a good choice of dog to be shown by children. Indeed, it can be quite amusing to see a young girl lifting her patient charge high onto the judge's table for assessment, often her own little face barely peeping above the dog's back, and yet the Cavalier seems to take this all in stride!

A Cavalier King Charles Spaniel is also a highly suitable breed to carry in a dog crate, something which is especially useful when traveling by car for this safety measure prevents the

Whether you lead an active lifestyle or a more sedentary one, your Cavalier will happily accompany you. Discuss your lifestyle with your breeder before selecting your puppy.

chance of escape when doors are opened or in case of accident. In short, the Cavalier is as handsome and portable a companion as anyone could desire. When seen with this compact, smart toy, you are undoubtedly traveling in style.

PERSONALITY
The Cavalier King Charles Spaniel can be equally at home with a large, boisterous family as he can with a single person, whatever that person's age. Having said that, children should always be instructed never to handle a dog too roughly, nor should they be permitted to tug at the coat. The breed can be happy living with energetic owners who are likely to take their dog out on long, exciting walks, but can also live a comfortable and happy life

following a more sedentary existence. When living with a less active family, the dog must be afforded ample opportunity for exercise and activity to avoid obesity. This is a factor that must be considered when taking on any breed of dog.

The amenable Cavalier will generally adapt to whatever lifestyle is offered and will adapt readily to a regular short walk around the block, a longer walk with a free romp in the park, or merely a good energetic game with a ball in your backyard. At other times of day the Cavalier will be quite content to join his owner watching the TV, curled up on the sofa or resting comfortably in a corner of the sitting room. The Cavalier is a breed that is often described as "a people dog," one that appreciates, enjoys and indeed needs human company.

The Cavalier King Charles Spaniel generally gets along well with other dogs and household pets, rarely showing any particular jealousy or possessiveness over tidbits or favorite toys. Of course, when introducing any dog to a new companion, caution must be exercised on the part of the owner, but in the case of Cavaliers such introduction is rarely stressful for any party concerned. Like many other breeds, Cavaliers seem to thoroughly enjoy the company

Cavalier King Charles Spaniels are as handsome as they are personable and loving. Given the proper training and attention, the Cavalier can delight most anyone!

of other dogs. Many owners like to keep a couple of Cavaliers as pets, as they make for happy companionship and are so easy to look after. Owning and caring for two requires little more work than just one. Although no dog owner should regularly leave dogs alone for long periods, a Cavalier will usually appreciate the company of a canine companion if his owner does have to be away from home for a few hours from time to time.

This is not a breed of dog that should be left outside all day in a kennel. Instead it is a pet, a canine companion that prefers to be involved in human activity so should be allowed to live within the household as a family companion, however large or small the family. In the mind of an adoring dog, one owner is quite sufficient as a family, provided that person gives him every care and attention he needs and deserves.

Cavaliers are happy to be followers. Except when hunting, the Cavalier is not really a very independent breed, but instead is one which prefers to rely on a pack leader and, of course, the pack leader is, or should be, the dog's owner.

We all know that there are exceptions to every rule, but the Cavalier is not what might be described as a "yappy" dog. Like most dogs, the Cavalier will bark if there is a stranger about.

Despite this, the Cavalier is not suitable as a guarding breed for its very nature is too soft to deter any intruder and he's a little small to pose any real threat.

Although there are certainly Cavaliers that are obedience trained, many owners claim their dogs have absolutely no road sense, so it is always wise to walk your dog on a lead in any public place, which may be a law in your community. Although the Cavalier does not have the long legs of breeds like the Whippet or Greyhound, it is surprising how quickly those little legs can move. One must always be aware that the safety of one's dog is of paramount importance and that a dog on the loose in the wrong place can also cause danger to others and cause traffic accidents.

COLORS AND COAT

Apart from the breed's attractiveness in ease of size, management and personality, it is the Cavalier's glorious array of colors that endears many people to this breed. The range of colors now includes Blenheim, Ruby, Black

A LONG AND HAPPY LIFE
Most smaller breeds of dog tend to live longer than very large, heavy ones. The Cavalier King Charles Spaniel can be expected to live on average for 11 to 12 years, sometimes longer.

and Tan and Tricolor, of which the Blenheims are the most numerous. These are generally the easiest to obtain for when a dog and bitch of this color are mated together they always produce Blenheims, no matter what other colors are involved in the genetic background. Certainly the Blenheims with their rich tan and white markings are incredibly striking, and those that possess a lozenge mark on the head are very highly prized. Markings should, if possible, be evenly distributed on the head, and markings that are not symmetrical are likely to be penalized in the show ring.

Ideally both Blenheims and Tricolors should have their markings well broken up. Tricolors are black and white with tan markings over the eyes, on cheeks, inside the ears and legs, as well as on the underside of the tail. Again, a judge will look for the placement of these markings in a show dog. It is not always realized that the prized lozenge mark can also be found in Tricolors.

Black and tan can be yet another striking color combination. The black should be what is described as "raven black" and the tan markings should ideally be found above the eyes, on cheeks, inside ears, on chest, legs and the underside of the tail. These tan markings should be bright but any white found on the coat is undesirable. Technically, a Cavalier that is black and tan is described as a "whole color" and any white found in the coat would therefore

A Ruby Cavalier showing off his beautiful whole-colored rich red coat. Note there is not an undesirable speck of white on his coat.

be incorrect. There are not a great many black and tan Cavaliers to be found, so obtaining one of this color may indeed be difficult, or could involve a long wait. However, sometimes black and tans that show just a little white in their coat are available as pets for they would be penalized heavily in the show ring.

Rubies are whole colored in a rich red and, like black and tans, any white on the coat is undesirable. Having said that, sometimes ruby puppies are born with a small fleck of white on the head, but this will usually have disappeared by seven or eight months of age. Because, genetically, the ruby coloring is the most difficult to breed true, this color is not easily found.

Whatever the color of one's Cavalier, the coat will require regular grooming if it is to be kept in all its glory. Nonetheless, compared with some other breeds, the amount of grooming required is not excessive. The Cavalier is quite small and does not have as much coat as a Maltese or Rough Collie, for example.

Whether one decides to have a dog or a bitch as one's pet is very much a matter of personal preference and factors such as a bitch's coming into season will undoubtedly have some bearing on the final decision. However, it may also be worth bearing in mind that males do tend to have a little

more coat than females, which can make them rather more glamorous. Males may also need just a little more time spent in grooming than females. Conversely, a female Cavalier that has recently been in season will usually shed her coat. During this season, it is sensible management of the coat to keep one's pet in tip-top condition.

TAILS AND DEWCLAWS
Historically the docking of tails on Cavalier King Charles Spaniels has

been optional but, if done, it should have been carried out within the first few days of life and more than one-third of the tail should not have been removed. Docking of tails is now a subject under some debate, especially by the veterinary profession.

Dewclaws are usually removed, but again this must be done at a very early age, usually on the third or fourth day. Cavaliers rarely have dewclaws on the hind legs, but they should always be checked so that they are not left on unintentionally. The reason for removal of dewclaws is not just an esthetic consideration but avoids these claws, which are not functional in most breeds, from being torn when out running and exercising.

THE CAVALIER'S I.Q.

By normal canine standards, the Cavalier King Charles Spaniel has

The Cavalier requires daily brushing and combing to keep his soft and luxurious coat in good condition.

a fairly high I.Q. and many of his senses, such as smell and hearing, are more highly developed than those of humans. But even though a Cavalier fits in so well with home life, he, of course, does not, as some would like to believe, have near-human mentality. They are easily able to assimilate the fears and joys of their owners, so it follows that a somewhat nervous person may convey that feeling to the dog, which may well end up with a rather similar personality. Conversely, a highly boisterous or bubbly person is likely to end up with a Cavalier with a similar personality.

HEALTH CONSIDERATIONS

Many dogs, whatever their breed, suffer from health problems at some time during their lives, but undoubtedly some breeds seem more prone to certain problems than others. If well-informed, owners can be prepared to seek urgent veterinary advice so that any problems that may occur can be caught in the nick of time. This will facilitate a greater chance of recovery if possible, or management of the disease if it is one that is incurable.

Most Cavaliers are healthy little dogs but care must be taken to ensure that they do not put on too much weight. Because of the breed's appealing eyes, many are fed table scraps without sufficient thought. However, it is much

> ### A MINIATURE SNORTING BREED
>
> Not really a health problem, but something that can be perplexing and sometimes frightening for an owner is the breed's habit of snorting. This sounds rather like a choking cough but can easily be stopped by placing the hand over the dog's nose just for a few seconds. This causes the dog to open his mouth and clear the airway.

kinder to your dog in the long term to feed a healthy diet and keep treats only to sensible ones, certainly not chocolates and little pieces of cake, however tempting they may be! Obesity, however slight, can put additional stress on the heart, and some Cavaliers have a tendency to suffer from heart problems. Fortunately, many Cavaliers live long and healthy lives, but one should be aware that the apparent onset of heart conditions in the breed is usually around eight years, sometimes a little earlier.

Mitral valve disease, better known as MVD, is a very common heart disease in dogs, affecting smaller dogs as they get older. In the Cavalier, MVD can affect young dogs as well as old dogs. The disease, believed to be genetic in the Cavalier, affects the dog's heart mitral valve, which is responsible for correct blood flow from the atria to the ventricles. Vets can identify potential MVD victims

Occasionally Cavalier King Charles Spaniels also suffer from hereditary cataracts (HD) and multi-focal retinal dysplasia (MRD). The breed is currently under investigation for multi-ocular defects, which include any combination of nystagmus, microphthalmos, PPM, CHC and RD.

This all sounds rather alarming but good breeders have their stock screened for heart problems and are encouraged to have both parents eye tested prior to arranging a mating.

Because Cavaliers are fairly hardy dogs and can thoroughly enjoy a sporting life, they are also good water dogs. However, if a dog gets wet, especially in cold weather, it is essential to dry the coat so that the dog does not sit around for long periods feeling damp. This could lead to long-term joint problems, which might otherwise be avoided, not to mention possibly causing a chill!

through a murmur, the loudness of which increases as the leak in the dog's heart valve worsens.

There is no way to determine, currently, whether or not dogs with a murmur will develop MVD. Vets can use x-rays, ECG and ultrasounds to determine the severity of the disease. Affected dogs tire easily, breathe rapidly and possibly cough; fainting occurs in severe cases. Vets attempt to slow down the progress of the disease, but the unfortunate truth is that most Cavaliers who show heart problems will only live for up to two years. Breeders must have all Cavaliers checked regularly, as the genetic likelihood of the disease would preclude affected dogs from being bred.

A NATURAL BEAUTY

The Cavalier King Charles Spaniel has always been considered a natural breed and enthusiasts have tried hard to keep it that way. This has helped the Cavalier to remain an unexaggerated breed of dog, not one that requires great artistry in coat presentation for the show ring, although it must, of course, always be well groomed.

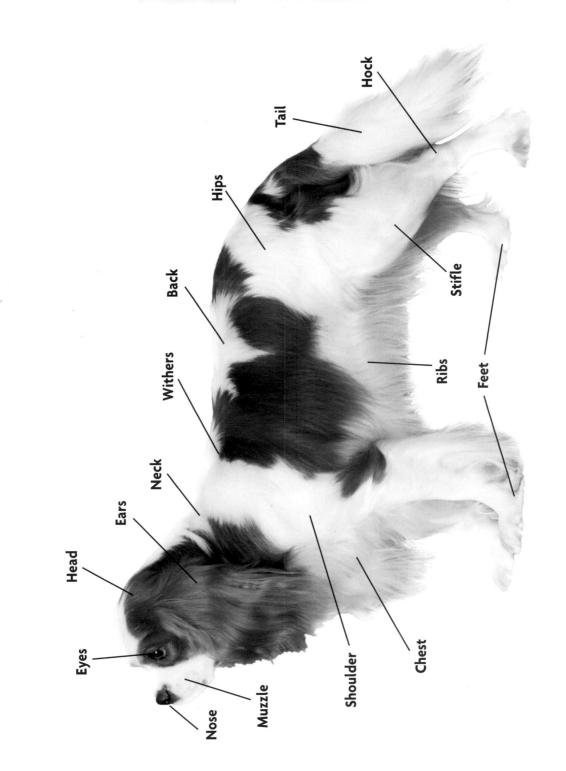

BREED STANDARD FOR THE

CAVALIER KING CHARLES SPANIEL

The breed standard for the Cavalier King Charles Spaniel is considered a "blue-print" for the breed. Effectively the various points of the dog are written down in such a way that a visual picture can be conjured up in one's mind. However, this is more easily said than done. Not only do standards vary slightly from country to country but people's interpretations of these breed standards vary also. This makes judges select different dogs for top honors, for each person's idea of which dog most closely fits the breed standard varies, albeit just slightly. That is not to say that a good dog does not win regularly under different judges, while an inferior dog may rarely even be placed at shows, at least not among quality competition. The breed standard given here is that accepted by the American Kennel Club.

AMERICAN KENNEL CLUB STANDARD FOR THE CAVALIER KING CHARLES SPANIEL

General Appearance: The Cavalier King Charles Spaniel is an active, graceful, well-balanced toy spaniel, very gay and free in action; fearless and sporting in character, yet at the same time gentle and affectionate. It is this typical gay temperament, combined with true elegance and royal appearance which are of paramount importance in the breed. Natural appearance with no trimming, sculpting or artificial alteration is essential to breed type.

Size, Proportion, Substance: *Size*—Height 12 to 13 inches at the withers; weight proportionate to height, between 13 and 18 pounds. A small, well balanced dog within these weights is desirable, but these are ideal heights and weights and slight variations are permissible. *Proportion*—The body approaches squareness, yet if measured from point of shoulder to point of buttock, is slightly longer than the height at the withers. The height from the withers to the elbow is approximately equal to the height from the elbow to the ground. *Substance*—Bone moderate in proportion to size. Weedy and coarse specimens are to be equally penalized.

The skull should appear almost flat between the ears.

Head: Proportionate to size of dog, appearing neither too large nor too small for the body. *Expression*—The sweet, gentle, melting expression is an important breed characteristic. *Eyes*—Large, round, but not prominent and set well apart; color a warm, very dark brown; giving a lustrous, limpid look. Rims dark. There should be cushioning under the eyes which contributes to the soft expression. *Faults*—Small, almond-shaped, prominent, or light eyes; white surrounding ring. *Ears*—Set high, but not close, on top of the head. Leather long with plenty of feathering and wide enough so that when the dog is alert, the ears fan slightly forward to frame the face. *Skull*—Slightly rounded, but without dome or peak; it should appear flat because of the high placement of the ears.

Stop is moderate, neither filled nor deep. *Muzzle*—Full muzzle slightly tapered. Length from base of stop to tip of nose about 1.5 inches. Face well filled below eyes. Any tendency towards snipiness undesirable. Nose pigment uniformly black without flesh marks and nostrils well developed. Lips well developed but not pendulous giving a clean finish. *Faults*—Sharp or pointed muzzles. *Bite*—A perfect, regular and complete scissors bite is preferred, i.e., the upper teeth closely overlapping the lower teeth and set square into the jaws. *Faults*—Undershot bite, weak or crooked teeth, crooked jaws.

Neck, Topline, Body: *Neck*—Fairly long, without throatiness, well enough muscled to form a slight arch at the crest. Set smoothly into nicely sloping shoulders to give an elegant look. *Topline*—Level both when moving and standing. *Body*—Short-coupled with ribs well spring but not barrelled. Chest moderately deep, extending to elbows allowing ample heart room. Slightly less body at the flank than at the last rib, but with no tucked-up appearance. *Tail*—Well set on, carried happily but never much above the level of the back, and in constant characteristic motion when the dog is in action. Docking is optional. If docked, no more than one third to be removed.

Forequarters: Shoulders well laid back. Forelegs straight and well under the dog with elbows close to the sides. Pasterns strong and feet compact with well-cushioned pads. Dewclaws may be removed.

Hindquarters: The hindquarters construction should come down from a good broad pelvis, moderately muscled; stifles well turned and hocks well let down. The hindlegs when viewed from the rear should parallel each other from hock to heel. *Faults*—Cow or sickle hocks.

Coat: Of moderate length, silky, free from curl. Slight wave permissible. Feathering on ears, chest, legs and tail should be long, and the feathering on the feet is a feature of the breed. No trimming of the dog is permitted. Hair growing between the pads on the underside of the feet may be trimmed.

Color: *Blenheim*—Rich chestnut markings well broken up on a clear, pearly white ground. The ears must be chestnut and the color evenly spaced on the head and surrounding both eyes, with a white blaze between the eyes and ears, in the center of which may be the lozenge or "Blenheim spot." The lozenge is a unique and desirable, though not essential, characteristic of the Blenheim. *Tricolor*—Jet black markings well broken up

on a clear, pearly white ground. The ears must be black and the color evenly spaced on the head and surrounding both eyes, with a white blaze between the eyes. Rich tan markings over the eyes, on cheeks, inside ears and on underside of tail. *Ruby*—Whole-colored rich red. *Black and Tan*—Jet black with rich, bright tan markings over eyes, on cheeks, inside ears, on chest, legs, and on underside of tail. *Faults*—Heavy ticking on Blenheims or Tricolors, white marks on Rubies or Black and Tans.

Gait: Free moving and elegant in action, with good reach in front and sound, driving rear action. When viewed from the side, the movement exhibits a good length of stride, and viewed from front and rear it is straight and true, resulting from straight-boned fronts and properly made and muscled hindquarters.

Cavaliers come in four color varieties. The standard describes precisely what comprises each color variety.

Temperament: Gay, friendly, non-aggressive with no tendency towards nervousness or shyness. Bad temper, shyness, and meanness are not to be tolerated and are to be severely penalized as to effectively remove the specimen from competition

AUTHOR'S COMMENTS

Let's take a closer look at some of the points in the standard. The nature of the breed as described under "Temperament" is really one of the highlights of the make-up of this thoroughly charming breed. In any good Cavalier, there should be no tendency toward nervousness so you can be reasonably sure that the puppy you buy has a friendly, outgoing character. Were a prospective purchaser to come across a Cavalier without good temperament, however beautiful it looks, it would be sensible to avoid that puppy as clearly the temperament would not fit the breed standard.

The skull of the Cavalier should appear almost flat between the ears, not domed as in the English Toy Spaniel or Chihuahua. The stop is the area of indentation between the eyes, where the nasal bone and skull meet.

Feathering is required on the ears as well as on the coat. This is the longer fringe of hair upon ears, legs, tail and body, just putting the finishing touches to a Cavalier in good coat.

The mouth of the Cavalier is to have a scissors bite, which means the upper incisors should close tightly over the lower ones. There should not be any significant gap between the upper and lower teeth or the bite would be overshot. Conversely, if the lower incisors overlap the upper ones, a fault that sometimes is found in the breed, this would be a reverse scissors bite. That the standard calls for a complete scissors bite means that the Cavalier should have a full complement of 42 teeth, with six upper and six lower incisors, these being the smaller teeth set at the front of the mouth between the large canines.

That the body is short-coupled means that the length of body between the end of the rib cage and the pelvic area is not too long, while a good spring of rib indicates that the ribs should have a reasonable degree of curvature. They should neither be too flat (known as "slab-sided"), nor overly rounded (known usually as "barrelled").

The length of the tail should be in balance with the body. This is one of the reasons why, if the tail is docked, not more than a third of the length is removed. If the tail were too short, it would consequently be out of balance with the rest of the dog. When moving, the tail is carried happily but never carried above the level of the back.

HEAD
The head is almost flat between the ears (left); it should never appear domed (right).

MUZZLE
The muzzle should be slightly tapered, about 1.5 inches in length with a moderate stop (left). It should neither be too long (center) nor too short (right).

EYES
The eyes should be large and round but not too prominent.

HINDQUARTERS
The hindquarters have well-turned stifles (left), never turning inward (cowhocks, right).

TAIL
The tail is well set on and carried happily (left), but never much above the level of back (right).

FEET
The feet should be compact and well feathered (left). Toes should not be splayed (right).

CAVALIER KING CHARLES SPANIEL

Visit the breeder to view the litter and the parents. Surely your child will be happy to help make the selection.

You have probably decided on a Cavalier King Charles Spaniel as your choice of pet following a visit to the home of a friend or acquaintance, where you have seen an adorable Cavalier looking gloriously elegant on the sofa. This certainly makes for a pretty picture, but as a new owner you must realize that a good deal of care, commitment and training goes into raising a boisterous puppy so that your pet turns into a well-behaved adult.

In deciding to take on a new puppy, you will be committing yourself to around 12 years of responsibility. No dog should be discarded after a few months or even a few years when the novelty has worn off. Instead, your

PROCEED WITH CAUTION

When breeds become very popular, and such is the case with the Cavalier, although there are many truly dedicated breeders, there become an increasing number of less reputable ones too. It is therefore essential to select a breeder with the very greatest of care.

Cavalier King Charles Spaniel should be joining your household to spend the rest of his days with you.

Although a Cavalier is much easier to look after than many other breeds, you will still need to carry out a certain amount of training. Unlike some of the larger breeds, the Cavalier will not respond well to overly strict training. Instead you will need to take a firm but gentle approach in order to get the very best out of your pet.

A Cavalier generally likes to be clean around the house, but you will need to teach your puppy what is and is not expected. You will need to be consistent in your instructions; it is no good accepting certain behavior one day and not the next; your puppy simply will not understand and will be utterly confused. Your Cavalier will want to please you, so you will need to demonstrate clearly how your puppy is to achieve this.

Although the dog you are taking into your home will be fairly small and therefore probably less troublesome than a large dog, there undoubtedly will be a period of settling in. This will be great fun but you must be prepared for mishaps around the home during the first few weeks of your life together. It will be important that breakables are kept well out of harm's way and you will have to think twice about where you place hot cups of coffee or anything breakable. Accidents can and do happen, so you will need to think ahead so as to avoid these. Electric cords must be carefully concealed and your puppy must be taught where and where not to go.

Before making your commitment to a new puppy, do also think carefully about your future vacation plans. If you have thought things through carefully, discussed the matter thoroughly with all the members of your household, you will come to the right decision. If you decide that a Cavalier should join your family this will be a happy, long-term relationship for all parties concerned.

ARE YOU PREPARED?

Unfortunately, when a puppy is bought by someone who does not take into consideration the time and attention that dog ownership requires, it is the puppy who suffers when he is either abandoned or placed in a shelter by a frustrated owner. So all of the "homework" you do in preparation for your pup's arrival will benefit you both. The more informed you are, the more you will know what to expect and the better equipped you will be to handle the ups and downs of raising a puppy. Hopefully, everyone in the household is willing to do his part in raising and caring for the pup. The anticipation of owning a dog often brings a lot of promises from excited family members: "I will walk him every day," "I will feed him," "I will house-train him," etc., but these things take time and effort, and promises can easily be forgotten once the novelty of the new pet has worn off.

BUYING THE CAVALIER PUPPY

Although you may be looking for a Cavalier King Charles Spaniel as a pet rather than as a show dog, this does not mean that you want a dog that is in any way "second-rate." A caring breeder will have brought up the entire litter of puppies with the same amount of dedication. Thus, a puppy destined for a pet home should be just as healthy and outgoing as the one that hopes to end up in the show ring.

Because you have carefully selected this breed, you will want a Cavalier that is a typical specimen, both in looks and in temperament. In your endeavors to find such a puppy, you will have to select the breeder with care. The American

TEMPERAMENT COUNTS
Your selection of a good puppy can be determined by your needs. A show potential or a good pet? It is your choice. Every puppy, however, should be of good temperament. Although show-quality puppies are bred and raised with emphasis on physical conformation, responsible breeders strive for equally good temperament. Do not buy from a breeder who concentrates solely on physical beauty at the expense of personality.

Kennel Club will almost certainly be able to give you names of contacts within Cavalier breed clubs. These members can possibly put you in touch with breeders who may have puppies for sale. However, although these people can point you in the right direction, it will be up to you to do your home-work carefully.

Even though you may not be looking for a show dog, it is always a good idea to visit a show so that you can see quality speci-mens of the breed. This will also give you an opportunity to meet breeders who will probably be able to answer some of your queries. In addition, you will get some idea about which breeders appear to take most care of their stock, and which are likely to have given their puppies the best possible start in life. Something else you may be able to decide upon is which color appeals to you most, though the ruby and black and tan will be more diffi-cult to acquire than the Blenheim or tricolor.

When buying your puppy you will need to know about vaccina-tions, those already given and those still due. It is important that any injections already given by a veterinarian have documentary evidence to prove this. A worm-ing routine is also vital for any young puppy, so the breeder should be able to tell you exactly.

what treatment has been given, when it was administered and how you should continue.

PUPPY APPEARANCE

You should not even think about buying a puppy that looks sick, under-nourished, overly frightened or nervous. Sometimes a timid puppy will warm up to you after a 30-minute "let's-get-acquainted" session.

Your puppy should have a well-fed appearance but not a distended abdomen, which may indicate worms or incorrect feeding, or both. The body should be firm, with a solid feel. The skin of the abdomen should be pale pink and clean, without signs of scratching or rash. Check the hind legs to make certain that dewclaws were removed.

Clearly when selecting a puppy, the one you choose must be in good condition. The coat should look glossy and there should be no discharge from eyes or nose. Ears should also be clean, and of course there should be absolutely no sign of parasites. Check that there is no rash on the skin, and of course the puppy you choose should not have evidence of loose motions.

As in several other breeds, some Cavalier puppies have umbilical hernias, which can be seen as a small lump on the tummy where the umbilical cord was attached. Clearly it is prefer-able not to have such a hernia on any puppy, but you should check for this at the outset and if there is one you should discuss the seri-ousness of this with the breeder.

Most umbilical hernias are safe but your vet should keep an eye on this in case an operation is needed.

Finally a few words of warning. Never under any circumstances buy a puppy from a retail outlet, however clean or well managed it may appear. Nor should you buy through a third party, something which happens all too often and may not even be realized by the purchaser. Always insist that you see the puppy's dam and, if possible, the sire. Frequently the sire will not be owned by the breeder of the litter, so a photograph should be available for you to see. Ask if the breeder has any other of the puppy's relations for you to meet; for example there may be an older half-sister or half-brother. It would be beneficial for you to see how they have turned out, their mature size, coat quality, temperament and so on.

Be sure, too, that if you decide to buy a puppy, all relevant sales documentation is provided at the time of sale. You will need a copy of the pedigree, AKC registration documents, vaccination certificates, health guarantee and a feeding chart so that you know exactly how the puppy has been fed and how you should continue. Some careful breeders provide their puppy buyers with a small amount of food so that there is no risk of an upset tummy, allowing for a gradual change of diet if such is necessary.

COMMITMENT OF OWNERSHIP
After considering all of these factors, you have most likely made some very important decisions about selecting your puppy. You have chosen a Cavalier King

PEDIGREE VS. REGISTRATION CERTIFICATE

Too often new owners are confused between these two important documents. Your puppy's pedigree, essentially a family tree, is a written record of a dog's genealogy of three generations or more. The pedigree will show you the names as well as performance titles of all dogs in your pup's background. Your breeder must provide you with a registration application, with his part properly filled out. You must complete the application and send it to the AKC with the proper fee. Every puppy must come from a litter that has been AKC-registered by the breeder, born in the US and from a sire and dam that are also registered with the AKC.

The seller must provide you with complete records to identify the puppy. The AKC requires that the seller provide the buyer with the following: breed; sex, color and markings; date of birth; litter number (when available); names and registration numbers of the parents; breeder's name; and date sold or delivered.

Who's having more fun...the child or the puppies? If children are going to live with the Cavalier puppy, they should meet before you make the purchase. The way this photo looks, making a selection is going to be very difficult.

Charles Spaniel, which means that you have decided which characteristics you want in a dog and what type of dog will best fit into your family and lifestyle. If you have selected a breeder, you have gone a step further—you have done your research and found a responsible, conscientious person who breeds quality Cavaliers and who should be a reliable source of help as you and your puppy adjust to life together. If you have observed a litter in action, you have obtained a firsthand look at the dynamics of a puppy "pack" and, thus, you should learn about each pup's individual personality—perhaps you have even found one that particularly appeals to you.

However, even if you have not yet found the Cavalier puppy of your dreams, observing pups will help you learn to recognize certain behavior and to determine what a pup's behavior indicates about his temperament. You will be able to pick out which pups

TIME TO GO HOME

Breeders rarely release puppies until they are 10 to 12 weeks of age. This is an acceptable age for toy breeds, which are kept longer than other pups, given their petite sizes. If a breeder has a puppy that is 12 weeks of age or older, he is likely well socialized and house-trained. Be sure that he is otherwise healthy before deciding to take him home.

You should always see the dam with her puppies. It is quite usual to select the puppy of your choice when it is still very young and then come to take the puppy home when it is 10 to 12 weeks old.

are the leaders, which ones are less outgoing, which ones are confident, which ones are shy, playful, friendly, aggressive, etc. Equally as important, you will learn to recognize what a healthy pup should look and act like. All of these things will help you in your search, and when you find the Cavalier that was meant for you, you will know it!

Researching your breed, selecting a responsible breeder and observing as many pups as possible are all important steps on the way to dog ownership. It may seem like a lot of effort…and you have not even brought the pup home yet! Remember, though, you cannot be too careful when it comes to deciding on the type of dog you want and finding out about your prospective pup's background. Buying a puppy is not—or should not be—just another whimsical purchase. This is one instance in which you actually do get to choose your own

YOUR SCHEDULE . . .

If you lead an erratic, unpredictable life, with daily or weekly changes in your work requirements, consider the problems of owning a puppy. The new puppy has to be fed regularly, socialized (loved, petted, handled, introduced to other people) and, most importantly, allowed to go outdoors for house-training. As the dog gets older, he can be more tolerant of deviations in his feeding and relief schedule.

family! You may be thinking that buying a puppy should be fun—it should not be so serious and so much work. Keep in mind that your puppy is not a cuddly stuffed toy or decorative ornament, but a creature that will become a real member of your family. You will come to realize that, while buying a puppy is a pleasurable and exciting endeavor, it is not something to be taken lightly. Relax...the fun will start when the pup comes home!

Always keep in mind that a puppy is nothing more than a baby in a furry disguise...a baby who is virtually helpless in a human world and who trusts his owner for fulfillment of his basic needs for survival. In addition to food, water and shelter, your pup needs care, protection, guidance and love. If you are not prepared to commit to this, then you are not prepared to own a dog.

"A baby in a furry disguise" accurately describes this Cavalier angel.

ARE YOU A FIT OWNER?

If the breeder from whom you are buying a puppy asks you a lot of personal questions, do not be insulted. Such a breeder wants to be sure that you will be a fit provider for his puppy.

"Wait a minute", you say. "How hard could this be? All of my neighbors own dogs and they seem to be doing just fine. Why should I have to worry about all of this?" Well, you should not worry about it; in fact, you will probably find that once your Cavalier pup gets used to his new home, he will fall into his place in the family quite naturally. But it never hurts to emphasize the commitment of dog ownership. With some time and patience, it is really not too difficult to raise a curious and exuberant Cavalier pup to be a well-adjusted and well-mannered adult dog—a dog that could be your most loyal friend.

Durable and portable! Be careful in handling your Cavalier. These three do not seem too disconcerted by their enthusiastic handler.

PREPARING PUPPY'S PLACE IN YOUR HOME

Researching your breed and finding a breeder are only two aspects of the "homework" you will have to do before bringing your Cavalier puppy home. You will also have to prepare your home and family for the new addition.

QUALITY FOOD

The cost of food must be mentioned. All dogs need a good-quality food with an adequate supply of protein to develop their bones and muscles properly. Most dogs are not picky eaters but, unless fed properly, can quickly succumb to skin problems.

Much as you would prepare a nursery for a newborn baby, you will need to designate a place in your home that will be the puppy's own. How you prepare your home will depend on how much freedom the dog will be allowed. Will he be confined to one room or a specific area in the house, or will he be allowed to roam as he pleases? Whatever you decide, you must ensure that he has a place that he can "call his own."

When you bring your new puppy into your home, you are bringing him into what will become his home as well. Obviously, you did not buy a puppy so that he could take over your house, but in order for a puppy to grow into a stable, well-adjusted dog, he has to feel comfortable in his surroundings. Remember, he is leaving the warmth and security of his dam and littermates, as well as the familiarity of the only place he has ever known, so it is important to make his transition as easy as possible. By preparing a place in your home for the puppy, you are making him feel as welcome as possible in a strange new place. It should not take him long to get used to it, but the sudden shock of being transplanted is somewhat traumatic for a young pup. Imagine how a small child would feel in the same situation—that is how your puppy must be feeling.

It is up to you to reassure him and to let him know, "Little fellow, you are going to like it here!"

WHAT YOU SHOULD BUY
CRATE

To someone unfamiliar with the use of crates in dog training, it may seem like punishment to shut a dog in a crate, but this is not the case at all. Crates are not cruel—crates have many humane and highly effective uses in dog care and training. For example, crate training is a very popular and very successful housebreaking method. A crate can keep your dog safe during travel; and, perhaps most importantly, a crate provides your dog with a place of his own in your home. It serves as a "doggie bedroom" of sorts—your Cavalier can curl up in his crate when he wants to sleep or when he just needs a break. Many dogs sleep in their crates overnight. With a crate mat and his favorite toy, a crate becomes a cozy pseudo-den for your dog. Like his ancestors, he too will seek out the comfort and retreat of a den—you just happen to be providing him with a safe, clean place to call his own.

As far as purchasing a crate, the type that you buy is up to you. It will most likely be one of the two most popular types: wire or fiberglass. There are advantages and disadvantages to each type. For example, a wire crate is more

PHOTO COURTESY OF MIKKI PET PRODUCTS.

open, allowing the air to flow through and affording the dog a view of what is going on around him, while a fiberglass crate is sturdier. Both can double as travel crates, providing protection for the dog. The size of the crate is another thing to consider. Puppies do not stay puppies forever but Cavaliers do not increase too

Your local pet shop should have a variety of crates in various sizes and styles. A crate is the first thing you should buy for your new puppy.

Your Cavalier will accept his crate as his own special place in no time.

greatly in size so you should easily be able to select a medium crate that will last into adulthood.

BEDDING

A crate mat in the dog's crate will help the dog feel more at home and in the cold months you can also give him a small blanket. This will take the place of the leaves, twigs, etc., that the pup would use in the wild to make a den; the pup can make his own "burrow" in the crate. Although your pup is far removed from his den-making ancestors, the denning instinct is still a part of his genetic makeup. Secondly, until you bring your pup home, he has been sleeping amid the warmth of his dam and littermates, and while a blanket is not the same as a warm, breathing body, it still provides heat and something with which to snuggle. You will want to wash your pup's blankets frequently in case he has an accident in his crate, and replace or remove any blanket that becomes ragged and starts to fall apart.

Your puppy has just left the warmth of his littermates. Don't expect him to adjust to his life as an only child overnight. This is a giant adjustment for such a little creature.

TOYS

Toys are a must for dogs of all ages, especially for curious playful pups. Puppies are the "children" of the dog world, and what child does not love toys? Chew toys provide enjoyment to both dog and owner—your dog will enjoy playing with his favorite toys, while you will enjoy the fact that they distract him from your expensive shoes and leather sofa. Puppies love to chew; in fact, chewing is a physical need for pups as they are teething, and everything looks appetizing! The full range of your possessions— from old dishcloth to Oriental rug—are fair game in the eyes of a teething pup. Puppies are not all that discerning when it comes to finding something to literally "sink their teeth into"—everything tastes great!

Cavalier puppies like to chew so you should offer them safe, durable toys made especially for dogs. Breeders advise owners to resist stuffed toys, because they can become de-stuffed in no time.

LEAD

A nylon lead is probably the best option as it is the most resistant to puppy teeth should your pup take a liking to chewing on his lead. Of course, this is a habit that should be nipped in the bud, but if your pup likes to chew on his lead he has a very slim chance of being able to chew through the strong nylon. Nylon leads are also light-weight, which is good for a young Cavalier who is just getting used to the idea of walking on a lead. For everyday walking and safety purposes, the nylon lead is a good choice. As your pup grows up and

Bedding is necessary for the crate. As picturesque as this puppy looks, you will have to offer your pup more than leaves to sleep on.

The overly excited pup may ingest the stuffing, which is neither digestible nor nutritious.

Similarly, squeaky toys are quite popular, but must be avoided for the Cavalier. Perhaps a squeaky toy can be used as an aid in training, but not for free play. If a pup "disembowels" one of these, the small plastic squeaker inside can be dangerous if swallowed. Monitor the condition of all your pup's toys carefully and get rid of any that have been chewed to the point of becoming potentially dangerous.

Be careful of natural bones, which have a tendency to splinter into sharp, dangerous pieces. Also be careful of rawhide, which can turn into pieces that are easy to swallow or into a mushy mess on your carpet.

CRATE-TRAINING TIPS

During crate training, you should partition off the section of the crate in which the pup stays. If he is given too big an area, this will hinder your training efforts. Crate training is based on the fact that a dog does not like to soil his sleeping quarters, so it is inef-fective to keep a pup in an area that is so big that he can eliminate in one end and get far enough away from it to sleep. Also, you want to make the crate den-like for the pup. Blankets and a favorite toy will make the crate cozy for the small pup; as he grows, you may want to evict some of his "roommates" to make more room. It will take some coaxing at first, but be patient. Given some time to get used to it, your pup will adapt to his new home-within-a-home quite nicely.

gets used to walking on the lead, you may want to purchase a flexible lead. These leads allow you to extend the length to give the dog a broader area to explore or to shorten the length to keep the dog close to you. Of course there are special leads for training purposes, but these are not necessary for routine walks.

COLLAR

Your pup should get used to wearing a collar all of the time since you will want to attach his ID tags to it. You have to attach the lead to something! A lightweight nylon collar is a good choice; make sure that it fits snugly enough so that the pup cannot wriggle out of it, but is loose enough so that it will not be uncomfortably tight around the pup's neck. You should be able to fit a finger between the

pup and the collar. It may take some time for your pup to get used to wearing the collar, but soon he will not even notice that it is there. Choke collars are made for training, but should only be used by an experienced handler.

FOOD AND WATER BOWLS

Buy your Cavalier two sets of bowls for his food and water. Always select the best quality merchandise when shopping for your dog. Stainless steel or sturdy plastic bowls are popular choices. Plastic bowls are more chewable. Dogs tend not to chew on the steel variety, which can be sterilized. It is important to buy sturdy bowls since anything is in danger of being chewed by puppy teeth and you do not want your dog to be constantly chewing apart his bowl (for his safety and for your purse!).

Your local pet shop should have an interesting variety of toys made especially for dogs. Never use human toys for dogs as they may be dangerous to a puppy.

TOYS, TOYS, TOYS!

With a big variety of dog toys available, and so many that look like they would be a lot of fun for a dog, be careful in your selection. It is amazing what a set of puppy teeth can do to an innocent-looking toy, so, obviously, safety is a major consideration. Be sure to choose the most durable products that you can find. Hard nylon bones and toys are a safe bet, and many of them are offered in different scents and flavors that will be sure to capture your dog's attention. It is always fun to play a game of fetch with your dog, and there are balls and flying discs that are specially made to withstand dog teeth.

CLEANING SUPPLIES

Until a pup is house-trained, you will be doing a lot of cleaning. Accidents will occur, which is okay in the beginning because the puppy does not know any better. All you can do is be prepared to clean up any accidents. Old rags, towels, newspapers and a safe disinfectant are good to have on hand.

BEYOND THE BASICS

The items previously discussed are the bare necessities. You will find out what else you need as you go along—grooming supplies, flea/tick protection, baby gates to partition a room,

The buckle collar is the standard collar used for everyday purposes. Be sure that you adjust the buckle on growing puppies. Check it every day. It can become too tight overnight! These collars can be made of leather or nylon. Attach your dog's identification tags to this collar.

The choke chain is the usual collar recommended for training. It is constructed of highly polished steel so that it slides easily through the stainless steel loop. The idea is that the dog controls the pressure around his neck and he will stop pulling if the collar becomes uncomfortable. The chain choke can damage the Cavalier's coat, so try a nylon or cotton one.

The halter is for a trained dog that has to be restrained to prevent running away, chasing a cat and the like. Considered the most humane of all collars, it is frequently used on smaller dogs for which collars are not comfortable.

etc. These things will vary depending on your situation but it is important that you have everything you need to feed and make your Cavalier comfortable in his first few days at home.

PUPPY-PROOFING YOUR HOME
Aside from making sure that your Cavalier will be comfortable in your home, you also have to make sure that your home is safe for your Cavalier. This means taking precautions that your pup will not get into anything he should not get into and that there is nothing within his reach that may harm him should he sniff it, chew it, inspect it, etc. This probably seems obvious since, while you are primarily concerned with your pup's safety, at the same time you do not want your belongings to be ruined. Breakables should be placed out of reach if your dog is to have full run of the house. If he is to be limited to certain places within the house, keep any potentially dangerous items in the "off-limits" areas. An electrical cord can pose a danger should the puppy decide to taste it—and who is going to convince a pup that it would not make a great chew toy? Cords should be fastened tightly against the wall. Always make sure that there is nothing near his crate that he can reach if he sticks his curious little nose or paws through the

openings. Just as you would with a child, keep all household cleaners and chemicals where the pup cannot get to them.

It is also important to make sure that the outside of your home is safe. Of course your puppy should never be unsupervised, but a pup let loose in the yard will want to run and explore, and he should be granted that freedom. Do not let a fence give you a false sense of security; you would be surprised how crafty (and persistent) a dog can be in figuring out how to dig under and squeeze his way through small holes, or to

Make sure your home is safe for your Cavalier. He depends on you for his safety and well-being.

Your pet shop will have a large selection of leads in all colors, materials, lengths, strengths and prices.

FINANCIAL RESPONSIBILITY

Grooming tools, collars, leashes, crate, dog beds and, of course, toys will be expenses to you when you first obtain your pup, and the cost will continue throughout your dog's lifetime. If your puppy damages or destroys your possessions (as most puppies surely will!) or something belonging to a neighbor. you can calculate additional expense. There is also flea and pest control, which every dog owner faces more than once. You must be able to handle the financial responsibility of owning a dog.

Your local pet shop will have a large selection of food and water bowls from which you can select the one that best suits your needs.

HOME SAFETY

Thoroughly puppy-proof your house before bringing your puppy home. Never use roach or rodent poisons in any area accessible to the puppy. Avoid the use of toilet bowl cleaners. Most dogs are born with toilet bowl sonar and will take a drink if the lid is left open. Also keep the trash secured and out of reach.

Scour your carport for potential puppy dangers. Remove weed killers, pesticides and antifreeze materials. Antifreeze is highly toxic and even a few drops can kill an adult dog. The sweet taste attracts the animal, who will quickly consume it from the floor or curbside.

jump or climb over a fence. The remedy is to make the fence high enough so that it really is impossible for your dog to get over it (about 6 feet should suffice), and well embedded into the ground. Be sure to repair or secure any gaps in the fence. Check the fence periodically to ensure that it is in good shape and make repairs as needed; a very determined pup may return to the same spot to "work on it" until he is able to get through.

FIRST TRIP TO THE VET

You have picked out your puppy, and your home and family are ready. Now all you have to do is collect your Cavalier from the breeder and the fun begins, right? Well...not so fast. Something else you need to prepare is your pup's first trip to the veterinarian. Perhaps the breeder can recommend someone in the area who specializes in toy breeds, or maybe you know some other Cavalier owners who can suggest a good vet. Either way, you should have an appointment arranged for your pup before you pick him up and plan on taking him for an examination before bringing him home.

Pet shops sell scooping devices that can make your chores easier and more sanitary.

NATURAL TOXINS

Examine your grass and landscaping before bringing your puppy home. Many varieties of plants have leaves, stems or flowers that are toxic if ingested, and you can depend on a curious puppy to investigate them.

If you see your dog carrying a piece of vegetation in his mouth, approach him in a quiet, disinterested manner, avoid eye contact, pet him and gradually remove the plant from his mouth. Alternatively, offer him a treat and maybe he'll drop the plant on his own accord. Be sure no toxic plants are growing in your own yard or kept in your home. Ask your vet for information on poisonous plants or research them at your library.

The pup's first visit will consist of an overall examination to make sure that the pup does not have any problems that are not apparent to you. The veterinarian will also set up a schedule for the pup's vaccinations; the breeder will inform you of which ones the pup has already received and the vet can continue from there.

INTRODUCTION TO THE FAMILY

Everyone in the house will be excited about the puppy's coming home and will want to pet him and play with him, but it is best

When offering your Cavalier puppy his first chew bone, make a fuss with soft words of endearment, petting and lots of loving attention.

him, as well as just putting him down and letting him explore on his own (under your watchful eye, of course).

The pup may approach the family members or may busy himself with exploring for a while. Gradually, each person should spend some time with the pup, one at a time, crouching down to get as close to the pup's level as possible and letting him sniff their hands and petting him gently. He definitely needs human attention and he needs to be touched—this is how to form an immediate bond. Just remember that the pup is experiencing a lot of things for the first time, at the same time. There are new people, new noises, new smells and new things to investigate: so be gentle, be affectionate and be as comforting as you can be.

to keep the introductions low-key so as not to overwhelm the puppy. He is apprehensive already. It is the first time he has been separated from his dam and the breeder, and the ride to your home is likely the first time he has been in a car. The last thing you want to do is smother him, as this will only frighten him further. This is not to say that human contact is not extremely necessary at this stage, because this is the time when a connection between the pup and his human family is formed. Gentle petting and soothing words should help console

THE RIDE HOME

Taking your dog from the breeder to your home in a car can be a very uncomfortable experience for both of you. The puppy will have been taken from his warm, friendly, safe environment and brought into a strange new environment—an environment that moves! Be prepared for loose bowels, urination, crying, whining and even fear biting. With proper love and encouragement when you arrive home, the stress of the trip should quickly disappear.

YOUR PUP'S
FIRST NIGHT HOME

You have traveled home with your new charge safely in his crate. He's been to the vet for a thorough check-up; he's been weighed, his papers examined; perhaps he's even been vaccinated and wormed as well. He's met the family, licked the whole family, including the excited children and the less-than-happy cat. He's explored his area, his new bed, the yard and anywhere else he's been permitted. He's eaten his first meal at home and relieved himself in the proper place. He's heard lots of new sounds, smelled new friends and seen more of the outside world than ever before.

That was just the first day! He's worn out and is ready for bed...or so you think!

It's puppy's first night and you are ready to say "Good night"—keep in mind that this is puppy's first night ever to be sleeping

Yes, you should demonstrate your affection for your Cavalier, but kissing on the mouth is not necessary.

Cavaliers tend to bond closely with one member of the family. They make devoted companions and alert watchdogs as well.

FEEDING TIPS

You will probably start feeding your pup the same food that he has been getting from the breeder; the breeder should give you a few days' supply to start you off. Although you should not give your pup too many treats, you will want to have puppy treats on hand for coaxing, training, rewards, etc. Be careful, though, as a small pup's calorie requirements are relatively low and a few treats can add up to almost a full day's worth of calories without the required nutrition.

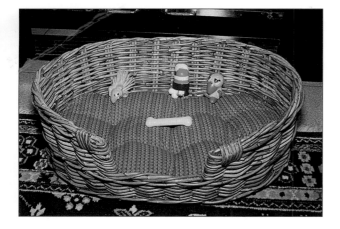

asleep without a peep. When the inevitable occurs, ignore the whining: he is fine. Be strong and keep his interest in mind. Do not allow your heart to become guilty and visit the pup. He will fall asleep.

Many breeders recommend placing a piece of bedding from his former homestead in his new bed so that he recognizes the scent of his littermates. Others still advise placing a hot water bottle in his bed for warmth. This latter may be a good idea provided the pup doesn't attempt to suckle—he'll get good and wet and may not fall asleep so fast.

Puppy's first night can be somewhat stressful for the pup and his new family. Remember that you are setting the tone of nighttime at your house. Unless you want to play with your pup every night at 10 p.m., midnight and 2 a.m., don't initiate the habit. Your family will thank you, and so will your pup!

You will need a bed and some toys to accommodate your Cavalier on his first night in his new home. Do your best to make the puppy comfortable, but don't overwhelm him all at once.

alone. His dam and littermates are no longer at paw's length and he's a bit scared, cold and lonely. Be reassuring to your new family member. This is not the time to spoil him and give in to his inevitable whining.

Puppies whine. They whine to let the others know where they are and hopefully to get company out of it. Place your pup in his new bed or crate in his room and close the door. Mercifully, he may fall

PREVENTING PUPPY PROBLEMS

SOCIALIZATION

Now that you have done all of the preparatory work and have helped your pup get accustomed to his new home and family, it is about time for you to have some fun! Socializing your Cavalier pup gives you the opportunity to show off your new friend, and your pup

All-day feeders are acceptable for adult dogs that are fully housebroken. Never use these feeders on puppies or on any Cavalier that tends to overeat.

gets to reap the benefits of being an adorable furry creature that people will want to pet and, in general, think is absolutely precious!

Besides getting to know his new family, your puppy should be exposed to other people, animals and situations, but of course he must not come into close contact with dogs you don't know well until his course of injections is fully completed. This will help him become well adjusted as he grows up and less prone to being timid or fearful of the new things he will encounter. Your pup's socialization began at the breeder's but now it is your responsibility to continue it. The socialization he receives up until the age of 12 weeks is the most critical, as this is the time when he forms his impressions of the outside world. Be especially careful at around the ten-week

period, also known as the fear period. The interaction he receives during this time should be gentle and reassuring. Lack of socialization can manifest itself in fear and aggression as the dog grows up. He needs lots of human contact, affection, handling and exposure to other animals.

Once your pup has received his necessary vaccinations, feel free to take him out and about (on his lead, of course). Walk him around the neighborhood, take him on your daily errands, let people pet him, let him meet other dogs and pets, etc. Puppies do not have to try to make friends; there will be no shortage of people who will want to introduce themselves. Just make sure

You can always use one of your pillows to make your Cavalier puppy comfortable. The smell of you on the pillow will aid in bonding. Be careful that the puppy doesn't rip the pillow open.

PUP MEETS WORLD

Thorough socialization includes not only meeting new people but also being introduced to new experiences such as riding in the car, having his coat brushed, hearing the television, walking in a crowd—the list is endless. The more your pup experiences, and the more positive the experiences are, the less of a shock and the less frightening it will be for your pup to encounter new things.

Socialization means getting along with others. The others usually include other dogs, cats and people. This Cavalier and his Rottweiler friend are sharing the same perch.

that you carefully supervise each meeting. If the neighborhood children want to say hello, for example, that is great—children and pups most often make great companions. Sometimes an excited child can unintentionally handle a pup too roughly, or an overzealous pup can playfully nip a little too hard. You want to make socialization experiences positive ones. What a pup learns during this very formative stage will impact his attitude toward future encounters. You want your dog to be comfortable around everyone. A pup that

has a bad experience with a child may grow up to be a dog that is shy around or aggressive toward children.

CONSISTENCY IN TRAINING
Dogs, being pack animals, naturally need a leader, or else they try to establish dominance in

It may be best to introduce your Cavalier to other dogs by using a puppy of another breed. The visiting puppy should neither be threatening nor overly dominant.

their packs. When you bring a dog into your family, the choice of who becomes the leader and who becomes the "pack" is entirely up to you! Your pup's intuitive quest for dominance, coupled with the fact that it is nearly impossible to look at an adorable Cavalier pup, with his "puppy-dog" face and not cave in, give the pup almost an unfair advantage in getting the upper hand! A pup will definitely test the waters to see what he can and cannot do. Do not give in to those pleading eyes—stand your ground when it comes to disciplining the pup and make sure that all family members do the same. It will only confuse the pup when Mother tells him to get off the couch when he is used to sitting up there with Father to watch the nightly news. Avoid discrepancies by having all members of the household decide on the rules before

Pure love and devotion are all the Cavalier knows. Nothing is as rewarding as bonding with your mistress.

the pup even comes home…and be consistent in enforcing them! Early training shapes the dog's personality, so you cannot be unclear in what you expect.

BOY OR GIRL?

An important consideration to be discussed is the sex of your puppy. For a family companion, a bitch may be the better choice, considering the female's inbred concern for all young creatures and her accompanying tolerance and patience. It is always advisable to spay a pet bitch or neuter a pet male, which may guarantee her a longer life.

COMMON PUPPY PROBLEMS

The best way to prevent puppy problems is to be proactive in stopping an undesirable behavior as soon as it starts. The old saying "You can't teach an old dog new tricks" does not necessarily hold true, but it is true that it is much easier to discourage bad behavior in a young developing pup than to wait until the pup's bad behavior becomes the adult dog's bad habit. There are some problems that are especially prevalent in puppies as they develop.

NIPPING

As puppies start to teethe, they feel the need to sink their teeth into anything available...unfortunately that includes your fingers, arms, hair and toes. You may find this behavior cute for the first five seconds...until you feel just how sharp those puppy teeth are. This is something you want to discourage immediately and consistently with a firm "No!" (or whatever number of firm "No's" it takes for him to understand that you mean business). Then replace your finger with an appropriate chew toy. While this behavior is merely annoying when the dog is young, it can become dangerous as your Cavalier's adult teeth grow in and his jaws develop, and he continues to think it is okay to gnaw on human appendages.

CRYING/WHINING

Your pup will often cry, whine, whimper, howl or make some other type of commotion when he is left alone. This is basically his way of calling out for attention to make sure that you know he is there and that you have not forgotten about him. He feels insecure when he is left alone, when you are out of the house

CHEWING TIPS

Chewing goes hand in hand with nipping in the sense that a teething puppy is always looking for a way to soothe his aching gums. In this case, instead of chewing on you, he may have taken a liking to your favorite shoe or something else that he should not be chewing. Again, realize that this is a normal canine behavior that does not need to be discouraged, only redirected. Your pup just needs to be taught what is acceptable to chew on and what is off-limits. Consistently tell him "No!" when you catch him chewing on something forbidden and give him a chew toy.

Conversely, praise him when you catch him chewing on something appropriate. In this way, you are discouraging the inappropriate behavior and reinforcing the desired behavior. The puppy's chewing should stop after his adult teeth have come in, but an adult dog continues to chew for various reasons—perhaps because he is bored, needs to relieve tension or just likes to chew. That is why it is important to redirect his chewing when he is still young.

and he is in his crate or when you are in another part of the house and he cannot see you. The noise he is making is an expression of the anxiety he feels at being alone, so he needs to be taught that being alone is okay. You are not actually training the dog to stop making noise, you are training him to feel comfortable when he is alone and thus removing the need for him to make the noise. This is where the crate with cozy bedding and toys comes in handy. You want to know that he is safe when you are not there to supervise, and you know that he will be safe in his crate rather than roaming freely about the house. In order for the pup to stay in his crate without making a fuss, he needs to be comfortable in his crate. On that note, it is extremely important that the crate is never used as a form of punishment, or the

pup will have a negative association with the crate.

Accustom the pup to the crate in short, gradually increasing time intervals in which you put him in the crate, maybe with a treat, and stay in the room with him. If he cries or makes a fuss, do not go to him, but stay in his sight. Gradually he will realize that staying in his crate is okay without your help, and it will not be so traumatic for him when you are not around. You may want to leave the radio on softly when you leave the house; the sound of human voices may be comforting to him.

Your Cav puppy's first day in your home can be scary. Be as gentle and supportive as you can be to make this transition as smooth as possible.

PUPPY PROBLEMS

The majority of problems that are commonly seen in young pups will disappear as your dog gets older. However, how you deal with problems when he is young will determine how he reacts to discipline as an adult dog. It is important to establish who is boss (ideally it will be you!) right away when you are first bonding with your dog. This bond will set the tone for the rest of your life together.

CAVALIER KING CHARLES SPANIEL

DIETARY AND FEEDING CONSIDERATIONS

Today the choices of food for your Cavalier King Charles Spaniel are many and varied. There are simply dozens of brands of food in all sorts of flavors and textures, ranging from puppy diets to those for seniors. There are even hypoallergenic and low-calorie diets available. Because your Cavalier's food has a bearing on coat, health and temperament, it is essential that the most suitable diet is selected for a Cavalier of his age. It is fair to say, however, that even experienced owners can be somewhat perplexed by the enormous range of foods available. Only understanding what is best for your dog will help you reach an informed decision.

Dog foods are produced in three basic types: dry, semi-moist and canned. Dry foods are useful for the cost-conscious for overall they tend to be less expensive than semi-moist or canned. These contain the least fat and the most preservatives. In general, canned foods are made up of 60-70% water, while semi-moist ones often contain so much sugar that they are perhaps the least preferred by owners, even though their dogs seem to like them. When selecting your dog's diet, three stages of development must be considered: the puppy stage, the adult stage and the senior stage.

Your Cavalier puppy will prosper on a well-balanced diet supplied by the usual dry food. Try feeding your Cav in his crate to encourage him to associate the crate with positive experiences.

PUPPY STAGE

Puppies instinctively want to suck milk from their mother's teats and a normal puppy will exhibit this behavior from just a few moments following birth. If puppies do not attempt to suckle within the first half-hour or so, they should be encouraged to do so by placing them on a nipple, having selected ones with plenty of milk. This early milk supply is important in providing colostrum to protect the puppies during the first eight to ten weeks of their lives. Although a mother's milk is much better than any milk formula, despite there being some excellent ones available, if the puppies do not feed the breeder will have to feed them himself. For those with less experience, advice from a veterinarian is important so that you feed not only the right quantity of milk but that of correct quality, fed at suitably frequent intervals, usually every two hours during the first few days of life.

Puppies should be allowed to nurse from their mother for about the first six weeks, although from the third or fourth week you will have begun to introduce small portions of suitable solid food. Most breeders like to introduce alternate milk and meat meals initially, building up to weaning time.

By the time the puppies are seven or a maximum of eight weeks old, they should be fully

Cavalier puppies instinctively want to suckle. Mother's milk contains elements that aid the puppy in early resistance to disease.

weaned and fed solely on a proprietary puppy food. Selection of the most suitable, good-quality diet at this time is essential for a puppy's fastest growth rate is during the first year of life. Veterinarians are usually able to offer advice in this regard and, although the frequency of meals will have

TEST FOR PROPER DIET

A good test for proper diet is the color, odor and firmness of your dog's stool. A healthy dog usually produces three semi-hard stools per day. The stools should have no unpleasant odor. They should be the same color from excretion to excretion.

The puppy's fastest growth is during his first year of life. Not all puppies grow at the same rate, nor do they all achieve the same size and weight.

been reduced over time, only when a young dog has reached the age of about 12 months should an adult diet be fed. Puppy and junior diets should be well balanced for the needs of your dog, so that except in certain circumstances additional vitamins, minerals and proteins will not be required.

ADULT DIETS

A dog is considered an adult when he has stopped growing, so in general the diet of a Cavalier can be changed to an adult one at about 10 to 12 months of age. Again you should rely upon your veterinarian or dietary specialist to recommend an acceptable maintenance diet. Major dog food manufacturers specialize in this type of food, and it is just necessary for you to select the one best suited to your dog's needs. Active

dogs may have different requirements than sedantary dogs.

SENIOR DIETS

As dogs get older, their metabolism changes. The older dog usually exercises less, moves

When you select a new puppy about ten weeks old, he should already be eating dry food.

more slowly and sleeps more. This change in lifestyle and physiological performance requires a change in diet. Since these changes take place slowly, they might not be recognizable. What is easily recognizable is weight gain. By continuing to feed your dog an adult-maintenance diet when he is slowing down metabolically, your dog will gain weight. Obesity in an older dog compounds the health problems that already accompany old age.

As your dog gets older, few of his organs function up to par. The kidneys slow down and the intestines become less efficient. These age-related factors are best handled with a change in diet and a change in feeding schedule to give smaller portions that are more easily digested.

There is no single best diet for every older dog. While many dogs do well on light or senior diets, other dogs do better on puppy diets or special premium diets such as lamb and rice. Be sensitive to your senior Cavalier's diet and this will help control other problems that may arise with your old friend.

WATER

Just as your dog needs proper nutrition from his food, water is an essential "nutrient" as well. Water keeps the dog's body properly hydrated and promotes normal function of the body's systems. During housebreaking, it is necessary to keep an eye on how much water your Cavalier is

GRAIN-BASED DIETS

Some less expensive dog foods are based on grains and other plant proteins. While these products may appear to be attractively priced, many breeders prefer a diet based on animal proteins and believe that they are more conducive to your dog's health. Many grain-based diets rely on soy protein, which may cause flatulence (passing gas).

There are many cases, however, when your dog might require a special diet. These special requirements should only be recommended by your veterinarian.

Cavaliers enjoy spending time with their owners, whether it's for grooming, exercise or just plain fun.

EXERCISE

Although a Cavalier King Charles Spaniel is small, all dogs require some form of exercise, regardless of breed. A sedentary lifestyle is as harmful to a dog as it is to a person. The Cavalier is a fairly active breed that enjoys exercise, but you don't have to be an Olympic athlete! Regular walks, play sessions in the yard or letting the dog run free in a safely enclosed area under your supervision are sufficient forms of exercise for the Cavalier. For those who are more ambitious, you will find that your Cavalier also enjoys long walks, an occasional hike or even a swim! This is more than a toy dog—he's a sporting dog at heart.

Bear in mind that an overweight dog should never be suddenly over-exercised; instead he should be allowed to increase exercise slowly. Not only is exercise essential to keep the dog's body fit, it is essential to his mental well-being. A bored dog will find something to do, which often manifests itself in some type of destructive behavior. In this sense, it is essential for the owner's mental well-being as well!

GROOMING

Even a Cavalier puppy will need to be groomed regularly so you should train him to enjoy short grooming sessions from a very early age. This will not involve a

drinking, but once he is reliably trained he should have access to clean fresh water at all times. Make sure that the dog's water bowl is clean, and change the water often, making sure that water is always available for your dog, especially if you feed dry food.

great deal of time, but ten minutes or so a day should be set aside. It is important that your puppy stands on a solid surface for grooming, a suitable table on which the dog will not slip. Under no circumstances should you leave your puppy Cavalier alone on a table for he may all too easily jump off and injure himself.

In adulthood, start grooming with your slicker brush, starting from the front and working towards the back of the dog. Leave the face and ears until last. Make sure that you pay particular attention to the areas that are most heavily coated. Always take care not to scratch the skin when

GROOMING EQUIPMENT

Always purchase the best quality grooming equipment so that your tools will last for many years to come. Here are some basics:

- Slicker brush
- Bristle brush
- Chamois
- Metal comb
- Scissors
- Rubber mat
- Dog shampoo
- Spray hose attachment
- Towels
- Blow dryer
- Ear cleaner
- Cotton balls
- Nail clippers
- Dental-care products

PHOTO COURTESY OF MIKKI PET PRODUCTS.

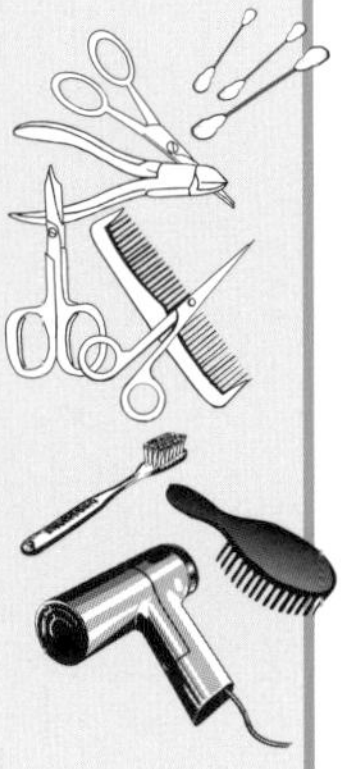

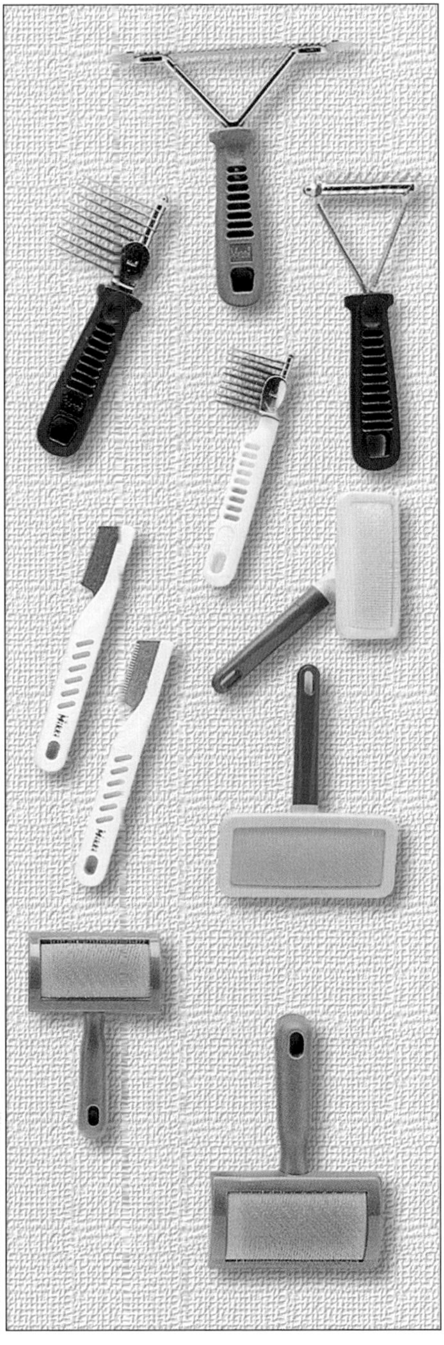

Your local pet shop will have a large supply of grooming tools from which you can choose. A slicker brush and flea comb are essential Cavalier tools.

Normal hairs of the Cavalier King Charles Spaniel enlarged 200 times original size. The inset shows the tip of a growing hair enlarged 2,000 times its original size.

SEM BY DR. DENNIS KINKEL, UNIVERSITY OF HAWAII

grooming and never tug at tangles; instead work at them slowly, just a few hairs at a time and soon enough they will have been eliminated without causing any pain or stress. The coat should then be brushed through with a bristle brush, always checking carefully under the tummy, "armpits" and behind the ears. You can finish off by using a fine-toothed comb.

Eyes and mouth should be wiped with a piece of damp cotton, tissue or piece of soft lint, then finished with chamois leather or silk. By grooming a little each day, or nearly every day, your Cavalier's coat should never become too problematic and dead hair will be removed as a matter of routine.

BATHING AND DRYING

The frequency with which you bathe your Cavalier will depend to a great extent on whether yours is a show dog or a pet. For the show ring, most exhibitors bathe their dogs before each show, perhaps as frequently as once a week. However, such frequent bathing is by no means essential, provided that the coat has been groomed in between times. The coat should have been groomed through before getting wet, but each owner tends to have his own tips as to how best to bathe. Personally I always like to stand my dogs on a non-slip mat in the

Your Cavalier should be brushed and combed regularly. If you begin grooming your Cav from puppyhood, he should accept grooming naturally as an adult. Be careful not to scratch the dog's skin with the comb.

The feathering should be done with a bristle brush. Always check the armpits, belly and behind the ears for possible mats.

The Cavalier's tail is done with a fine-toothed comb.

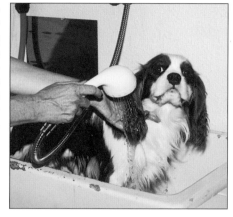

Check the temperature of the water before wetting your Cav. Use special dog shampoo. Never use human shampoo as it is too strong for a dog's skin.

When soaping the dog, be especially carefully around the Cav's eyes and ears. Nothing will convince a Cav that bathes are awful like soap in his eyes and water in his ears!

Use a blaster on low for the final drying process. Be extremely careful not to burn the dog.

bathtub and then wet the coat thoroughly using a shower-hose attachment. Always test the temperature of the water beforehand so that it is neither too hot nor too cold. Use a good quality shampoo designed especially for dogs. When this has been thoroughly rinsed off, apply a canine conditioner. You will probably find it best to use a gentler shampoo on the head so as to avoid any irritation to the eyes. It is also a good idea to put cotton balls in the ears to avoid water getting inside them but do, please, remember to take these out afterwards!

When the coat is completely rinsed with clean water, you can

BATHING BEAUTY

Once you are sure that the dog is thoroughly rinsed, squeeze the excess water out of his coat with your hand and dry him with an heavy towel. You may choose to use a blow dryer on his coat or just let it dry naturally. In cold weather, never allow your dog outside with a wet coat.

There are "dry bath" products on the market, which are sprays and powders intended for spot cleaning, that can be used between regular baths if necessary. They are not substitutes for regular baths, but they are easy to use for touch-ups as they do not require rinsing.

use highly absorbent towels to take off excess moisture and then take your dog out of the bath, wrapped in a clean towel. Undoubtedly your Cavalier will want to shake—so be prepared!

Drying can be done on whichever table you use for the grooming process. After a quick brushing, work over the coat systematically with the dryer, again neither too hot nor too cold, so always test it on your hand. You will find that few dogs like air blown directly onto their heads, so leave this until last. Although on a warm day you may be tempted to allow your dog to dry naturally, this will result in the coat curling more than you would wish, apart from which it takes longer so your dog is damp for quite a long while, even on a hot day.

At the end of a bathing session, both you and your

Most toy breeds have dental problems, including missing teeth and incorrect bites. Fortunately the Cav is fairly exceptional. Keep a close eye on your Cav's mouth.

Cleaning your Cavalier's teeth, preferably twice a week, is highly recommended to avoid plaque and tartar buildup.

SOAP IT UP

The use of human soap products like shampoo, bubble bath and hand soap can be damaging to a dog's coat and skin. Human products are too strong; they remove the protective oils coating the dog's hair and skin that make him water-resistant. Use only shampoo made especially for dogs. You may like to use a medicated shampoo, which will help to keep external parasites at bay.

Wrap your wet Cavalier in a heavy towel as soon as you have completed the rinsing phase.

Don't forget to let him shake off! If you don't dry the Cavalier thoroughly, be prepared for a shower all your own!

Ear cleaning should be done regularly. A cotton swab is not recommended as it can cause injury to the ear.

EAR CLEANING

The ears should be kept clean and any excess hair inside the ear should be carefully plucked out. Ears can be cleaned with a cotton ball and cleaner or ear powder made especially for dogs. Be on the lookout for any signs of infection or ear-mite infestation. If your Cavalier has been shaking his head or scratching at his ears frequently, this usually indicates a problem. If his ears have an unusual odor, this is a sure sign of mite infestation or infection and a signal to have his ears checked by the veterinarian.

NAIL CLIPPING

Your Cavalier should be accustomed to having his nails trimmed at an early age, since it will be a part of your maintenance routine throughout his life. Not only does

Cavalier will be pleased with the results and it is perhaps surprising how enjoyable this procedure can become once you have developed a routine.

it look nicer, but long, sharp nails can scratch someone unintentionally. Also, a long nail has a better chance of ripping and bleeding, or causing the feet to spread. A good rule of thumb is that if you can hear your dog's nails' clicking on the floor when he walks, his nails are too long.

Before you start cutting, make sure you can identify the "quick" in each nail. The quick is a blood vessel that runs through the center of each nail and grows rather close to the end. It will bleed if accidentally cut, which will be quite painful for the dog as it contains nerve endings. Keep some type of clotting agent on hand, such as a styptic pencil or styptic powder (the type used for shaving). This will stop the bleed-

PEDICURE TIP

A dog that spends a lot of time outside on a hard surface, such as cement or pavement, will have his nails naturally worn down and may not need to have them trimmed as often, except maybe in the colder months when he is not outside as much. Regardless, it is best to get your dog accustomed to the nail-trimming procedure at an early age so that he is used to it. Some dogs are especially sensitive about having their feet touched, but if a dog has experienced it since puppyhood, it should not bother him.

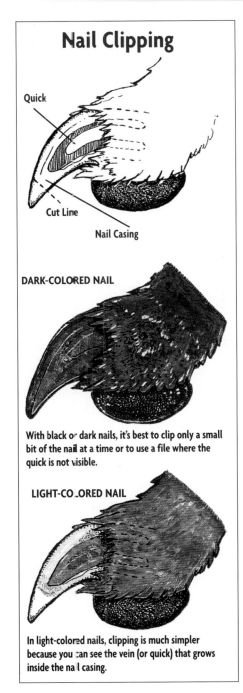

Nail Clipping

Quick

Cut Line

Nail Casing

DARK-COLORED NAIL

With black or dark nails, it's best to clip only a small bit of the nail at a time or to use a file where the quick is not visible.

LIGHT-COLORED NAIL

In light-colored nails, clipping is much simpler because you can see the vein (or quick) that grows inside the nail casing.

Use special dog nail clippers when trimming your Cavalier's nails.

ing quickly when applied to the end of the cut nail. Do not panic if this happens, just stop the bleeding and talk soothingly to your dog. Once your Cavalier has calmed down, move on to the next nail. It is better to clip a little at a time, particularly with black-nailed dogs.

Hold your pup steady as you begin trimming his nails; you do not want him to make any sudden movements or run away. Talk to him soothingly and stroke him as you clip. Holding his foot in your hand, simply take off the end of each nail in one quick clip. You can purchase nail clippers that are specially made for dogs; you can probably find them wherever you buy grooming supplies.

TRAVELING WITH YOUR DOG

CAR TRAVEL

You should accustom your Cavalier to riding in a car at an early age. You may or may not take him in the car often, but at the very least he will need to go to the vet and you do not want these trips to be traumatic for the dog or a big hassle for you. The safest way for a dog to ride in the car is in his crate. If he uses a crate in the house, you can use the same crate for travel.

Put the pup in the crate and see how he reacts. If he seems uneasy, you can have a passenger hold him on his lap while you drive. Another option is a specially made safety harness for dogs, which straps the dog in much like a seat belt. Do not let the dog roam loose in the vehicle—this is very dangerous! If you should stop short, your dog can be thrown and injured. If the dog starts climbing on you and pestering you while you are driving, you will not be able to concentrate on the road. It is an unsafe situation for every-one—human and canine.

For long trips, be prepared to stop to let the dog relieve himself. Bring along whatever you need to clean up after him. You should take along some paper towels and

MOTION SICKNESS

*If life is a motorway...*your dog may not want to come along for the ride! Some dogs experience motion sickness in cars that leads to excessive salivation and even vomiting. In most cases, your dog will fare better in the familiar safe confines of his crate. To desensitize your dog, try going on several short jaunts before trying a long trip. If your dog experiences distress when riding in the vehicle, drive with him only when absolutely necessary, and do not feed him or give him water before you go.

a bath towel for use should he have an accident in the car or suffer from motion sickness.

Never allow your Cavalier to move freely about your vehicle while you are driving. A simple crate is the safest place for the dog during traveling.

AIR TRAVEL

Contact your chosen airline before proceeding with your travel plans that include your Cavalier. The dog will be required to travel in a fiberglass crate and you should always check in advance with the airline regarding specific requirements. To help put the dog at ease, give him one of his favorite toys in the crate. Do not feed the dog for at least six hours before the trip in order to minimize his need to relieve himself. However,

TRAVEL TIP

Never leave your dog alone in the car. In hot weather, your dog can die from the high temperature inside a closed vehicle; even a car parked in the shade can heat up very quickly. Leaving the window open is dangerous as well since the dog can hurt himself trying to get out.

certain regulations specify that water must always be made available to the dog in the crate. Make sure your dog is properly identified and that your contact information appears on his ID tags and on his crate.

Discuss with your chosen airline whether or not your Cavalier can travel as a "carry-on." Many airlines offer this privilege to small-dog owners so that the dog can remain in the cabin with his owner. The crate must be able to fit under the passenger's seat. If the airline doesn't permit this kind of air travel, you are well advised to try a different airline.

BOARDING

So you want to take a family vacation—and you want to include all members of the family. You would probably make arrangements for accommodations ahead of time anyway, but this is especially important when traveling with a dog. You do not want to make an overnight stop at the only place around for miles and find out that they do not allow dogs. Also, you do not want to reserve a place for your family without confirming that you are traveling with a dog because if it is against their policy you may not have a place to stay.

Alternatively, if you are traveling and choose not to bring

A boarding kennel should have ample space for the Cavalier to exercise. Inspect the kennel before you use it. Look for cleanliness and the devotion of the staff.

your Cavalier, you will have to make arrangements for him while you are away. Some options are to take him to a neighbor's house to stay while you are gone, to have a trusted friend stop by often or stay at your house, or bring your dog to a reputable boarding kennel. If you choose to board him at a kennel, you should visit in advance to see the facility, how clean it is and where the dogs are kept. Talk to some of the employees and see how they treat the dogs—do they spend time with the dogs, play with them, exercise them, groom them, etc.? Also find out the kennel's policy on vaccinations and what they require. This is for all of the dogs' safety, since when dogs are kept together, there is a greater risk of diseases being passed from dog to dog.

IDENTIFICATION

Your Cavalier is your valued companion and friend. That is why you always keep a close eye on him and you have made sure that he cannot escape from the yard or wriggle out of his collar and run away from you. However, accidents can happen and there may come a time when your dog unexpectedly gets separated from you. If this unfortunate event should occur, the first thing on your mind will be finding him. Proper identification, including an ID tag, a tattoo and a microchip, will increase the chances of his being returned to you safely and quickly.

Tattooing inhibits the theft and loss of your beloved Cavalier. Some vets perform this service.

IDENTIFICATION OPTIONS

As puppies become more and more expensive, especially those puppies of high quality for showing and/or breeding, they have a greater chance of being stolen. The usual collar dog tag is, of course, easily removed. But there are two more permanent techniques that have become widely used for identification.

The puppy microchip implantation involves the injection of a small microchip, about the size of a corn kernel, under the skin of the dog. If your dog shows up at a clinic or shelter, or is offered for resale under less-than-savory circumstances, it can be positively identified by the microchip. The microchip is scanned, and a registry quickly identifies you as the owner.

Tattooing is done on various parts of the dog, from his belly to his ears. The number tattooed can be your telephone number, your dog's registration number or any other number that you can easily memorize. When professional dog thieves see a tattooed dog, they usually lose interest. For the safety of our dogs, no laboratory facility or dog broker will accept a tattooed dog as stock.

Discuss microchipping and tattooing with your veterinarian and breeder. Some vets perform these services on their own premises for a reasonable fee. To ensure that your dog's identification is effective, be certain that the dog is then properly registered with a legitimate national database.

Your Cavalier should always have a buckle collar with identification tags securely attached.

These Cavalier King Charles Spaniels are securely housed by a concrete surface and a heavy gate so they cannot wander away from home and become lost.

TRAINING YOUR

CAVALIER KING CHARLES SPANIEL

Living with an untrained dog is a lot like owning a piano that you do not know how to play—it is a nice object to look at but it does not do much more than that to bring you pleasure. Now try taking piano lessons and suddenly the piano comes alive and brings forth magical sounds and rhythms that set your heart singing and your body swaying.

The same is true with your Cavalier. Any dog is a big responsibility and if not trained sensibly may develop unacceptable behavior that annoys you or could even cause family friction.

To train your Cavalier, you may like to enroll in an obedi-ence class. Teach him good manners as you learn how and why he behaves the way he does. Find out how to communicate with your dog and how to recognize and understand his communications with you. Suddenly the dog takes on a new role in your life—he is smart, interesting, well behaved and fun to be with. He demonstrates his bond of devotion to you daily. In other words, your Cavalier does wonders for your ego because he constantly reminds you that you are not only his leader, you are his hero!

Those involved with teaching dog obedience and counseling owners about their dogs' behavior have discovered some interesting facts about dog ownership. For example, training dogs when they are puppies results in the highest rate of success in developing well-mannered and well-adjusted adult dogs. Training an older dog, from six months to six years of age, can produce almost equal results providing that the owner accepts the dog's slower rate of learning capability and is willing to work patiently to help the dog succeed

REAP THE REWARDS
If you start with a normal, healthy dog and give him time, patience and some carefully executed lessons, you will reap the rewards of that training for the life of the dog. And what a life it will be! The two of you will find immeasurable pleasure in the companionship you have built together with love, respect and understanding.

If you are attempting to train an older dog, you must accept the dog's slower rate of learning. Treats are a great assistance for puppy or adult dog alike.

at developing to his fullest potential. Unfortunately, many owners of untrained adult dogs lack the patience factor, so they do not persist until their dogs are successful at learning particular behaviors.

Training a puppy aged 10 to 16 weeks (20 weeks at the most) is like working with a dry sponge in a pool of water. The pup soaks up whatever you show him and constantly looks for more things to do and learn. At this early age, his body is not yet producing hormones, and therein lies the reason for such a high rate of success. Without hormones, he is focused on his owners and not particularly interested in investigating other places, dogs, people, etc. You are his leader: his provider of food, water, shelter and security. He latches onto you and wants to stay close. He will usually follow you from room to room, will not let you out of his sight when you are outdoors with him, and respond in like manner to the people and animals you encounter. If you greet a friend warmly, he will be happy to greet the person as well. If, however, you are hesitant, even anxious, about the approach of a stranger, he will respond accordingly.

PARENTAL GUIDANCE

Training a dog is a life experience. Many parents admit that much of what they know about raising children they learned from caring for their dogs. Dogs respond to love, fairness and guidance, just as children do. Become a good dog owner and you may become an even better parent.

Give your Cavalier puppy lots of encouragement and praise. All spaniels live to please their owners, and the tiny Cav is no exception.

Once the puppy begins to produce hormones, his natural curiosity emerges and he begins to investigate the world around him. It is at this time when you may notice that the untrained dog begins to wander away from you and even ignore your commands to stay close. When this behavior becomes a problem, the owner has two choices: get rid of the dog or train him. It is strongly urged that you choose the latter option.

There are usually classes within a reasonable distance from the owner's home, but you can also do a lot to train your dog yourself. Sometimes there are classes available but the tuition is too costly. Whatever the circumstances, the solution to training your dog without formal obedience classes lies within the pages of this book. This chapter is devoted to helping you train your Cavalier at home. If the recommended procedures are followed faithfully, you may expect positive results that will prove rewarding to both you and your dog.

Whether your new charge is a puppy or a mature adult, the methods of teaching and the techniques we use in training basic behaviors are the same. After all, no dog, whether puppy or adult, likes harsh or inhumane methods. All creatures, however, respond favorably to gentle motivational methods and sincere praise and encouragement. Now let us get started.

HOUSEBREAKING

You can train a puppy to relieve himself wherever you choose, but this location must be somewhere suitable. You should bear in mind from the outset that when your puppy is old enough to go out in

THINK BEFORE YOU BARK
Dogs are sensitive to their masters' moods and emotions. Use your voice wisely when communicating with your dog. Never raise your voice at your dog unless you are trying to correct him. "Barking" at your dog can become as meaningless as "dogspeak" is to you.

public places, any canine droppings must be removed at once. You will always have to carry with you a small plastic bag or "poop-scoop."

Outdoor training includes such surfaces as grass, dirt and cement. Indoor training usually means training your dog to newspaper. When deciding on the surface and location that you will want your Cavalier to use, be sure it is going to be permanent. Training your dog to grass and then changing your mind two months later is extremely difficult for both dog and owner.

Next, choose the command you will use each and every time you want your puppy to void. "Go hurry up" and "Potty" are examples of commands commonly used by dog owners.

MEALTIME

Mealtime should be a peaceful time for your puppy. Do not put his food and water bowls in a high-traffic area in the house. For example, give him his own little corner of the kitchen where he can eat undisturbed and where he will not be underfoot. Do not allow small children or other family members to disturb the pup when he is eating.

Get in the habit of giving the puppy your chosen relief command before you take him out. That way, when he becomes an adult, you will be able to determine if he wants to go out when you ask him. A confirmation will be signs of interest, including wagging his tail,

When puppies are led to soft grass, their natural instinct is to relieve themselves. They may sniff around in search of an area already utilized by a different dog.

When deciding on the surface of your Cav's relief area, be consistent. Cavaliers can be trained on grass, newspaper, cat litter, sand or something hard like slate or concrete. But once trained, they search for this same substrata to serve their needs.

watching you intently, going to the door, etc.

PUPPY'S NEEDS

Your new puppy needs to relieve himself after play periods, after each meal, after he has been sleeping and any time he indicates that he is looking for a place to urinate or defecate. The urinary and intestinal tract muscles of very young puppies are not fully developed. Therefore, like human babies, puppies need to relieve themselves frequently.

Take your puppy out often—every hour for an eight-week-old, for example, and always immediately after sleeping and eating. The older the puppy, the less often he will need to relieve himself. Finally, as a mature healthy adult, he will require only three to five relief trips per day.

HOUSING

Since the types of housing and control you provide for your puppy have a direct relationship

on the success of house-training, we consider the various aspects of both before we begin training.

Bringing a new puppy home and turning him loose in your house can be compared to turning a child loose in an amusement park and telling the child that the place is all his! The sheer enormity of the place would be too much for him to handle.

Instead, offer the puppy clearly defined areas where he can play, sleep, eat and live. A room of the house where the family gathers is the most obvious choice. Puppies are social animals and need to feel a part of the pack right from the start. Hearing your voice, watching you while you are doing things and smelling you nearby are all positive reinforcers that he is now a member of your pack. Usually a family room, the

THE CLEAN LIFE

By providing sleeping and resting quarters that fit the dog, and offering frequent opportunities to relieve himself outside his quarters, the puppy quickly learns that the outdoors (or the newspaper if you are training him to paper) is the place to go when he needs to urinate or defecate. It also reinforces his innate desire to keep his sleeping quarters clean. This, in turn, helps develop the muscle control that will eventually produce a dog with clean living habits.

kitchen or a nearby adjoining breakfast area is ideal for providing safety and security for both puppy and owner.

Within that room there should be a smaller area which the puppy can call his own. An alcove, a wire or fiberglass dog crate or a gated corner from which he can view the activities of his new family will be fine. The size of the area or crate is the key factor here. The area must be large enough for the puppy to lie down and stretch out as well as stand up without rubbing his head on the top, yet small enough so that he cannot relieve himself at one end and sleep at the other without coming into contact with his droppings. The designated area should be lined with clean bedding and a toy. Water must always be available, in a non-spill container.

Dogs are, by nature, clean animals and will not remain close to their relief areas unless forced to do so. In those cases, they then become dirty dogs and usually remain that way for life.

CONTROL

By *control*, we mean helping the puppy to create a lifestyle pattern that will be compatible to that of his human pack (*you!*). Just as we guide children to learn our way of life, we must show the puppy when it is time to play, eat, sleep, exercise and even entertain himself.

You puppy should always sleep in his crate. He should also learn that, during times of household confusion and excessive human activity such as at breakfast when family members are preparing for the day, he can play by himself in relative safety and comfort in his designated area.

After every nap, be sure the Cav puppy finds his way to his designated relief area.

PAPER CAPER

Never line your pup's sleeping area with newspaper. Puppy litters are usually raised on newspaper and, once in your home, the puppy will immediately associate newspaper with voiding. Never put newspaper on any floor while house-training, as this will only confuse the puppy. If you are paper-training him, use paper in his designated relief area only. Finally, restrict water intake after evening meals. Offer a few licks at a time—never let a young puppy gulp water after meals.

CANINE DEVELOPMENT SCHEDULE

It is important to understand how and at what age a puppy develops into adulthood. If you are a puppy owner, consult the following Canine Development Schedule to determine the stage of development your puppy is currently experiencing. This knowledge will help you as you work with the puppy in the weeks and months ahead.

Period	Age	Characteristics
FIRST TO THIRD	**BIRTH TO SEVEN WEEKS**	Puppy needs food, sleep and warmth, and responds to simple and gentle touching. Needs mother for security and disciplining. Needs littermates for learning and interacting with other dogs. Pup learns to function within a pack and learns pack order of dominance. Begin socializing pup with adults and children for short periods. Pup begins to become aware of his environment.
FOURTH	**EIGHT TO TWELVE WEEKS**	Brain is fully developed. Pup needs socializing with outside world. Remove from mother and littermates. Needs to change from canine pack to human pack. Human dominance necessary. Fear period occurs between 8 and 12 weeks. Avoid fright and pain.
FIFTH	**THIRTEEN TO SIXTEEN WEEKS**	Training and formal obedience should begin. Less association with other dogs, more with people, places, situations. Period will pass easily if you remember this is pup's change-to-adolescence time. Be firm and fair. Flight instinct prominent. Permissiveness and over-disciplining can do permanent damage. Praise for good behavior.
JUVENILE	**FOUR TO EIGHT MONTHS**	Another fear period about 7 to 8 months of age. It passes quickly, but be cautious of fright and pain. Sexual maturity reached. Dominant traits established. Dog should understand sit, down, come and stay by now.

NOTE: THESE ARE APPROXIMATE TIME FRAMES. ALLOW FOR INDIVIDUAL DIFFERENCES IN PUPPIES.

Wire crates provide more visual contact between you and the puppy. Cavs like to look around.

Each time you leave the puppy alone, he should understand exactly where he is to stay. Puppies are chewers. They cannot tell the difference between lamp cords, television wires, shoes, table legs, etc. Chewing into a television wire, for example, can be fatal to the puppy while a shorted wire can start a fire in the house.

If the puppy chews on the arm of the chair when he is alone, you will probably discipline him angrily when you get home. Thus, he makes the association that your coming home means he is going to be punished. (He will not remember chewing up the chair and is incapable of making the association of the discipline with his naughty deed.)

Other times of excitement, such as holidays, family parties, etc., can be fun for the puppy providing he can view the activities from the security of his designated area. He is not underfoot and he is not being fed all sorts of tidbits that will probably cause him stomach distress, yet he still feels a part of the fun.

SCHEDULE

A puppy should be taken to his relief area each time he is released from his designated area, after meals, after a play session, when he first awakens in the morning (at age eight weeks, this can mean 5 a.m.!). The puppy will indicate that he's ready "to go" by circling or sniffing busily—do not misinterpret these signs. For a puppy less than ten weeks of age, a routine of taking him out every hour is necessary. As the puppy grows, he will be able to wait for longer periods of time.

Keep trips to his relief area short. Stay no more than five or six minutes and then return to the house. If he goes during that time, praise him lavishly and take him indoors immediately. If he does not, but he has an accident when you go back indoors, pick him up immediately, say "No! No!" and return to his relief area. Wait a few minutes, then return to the

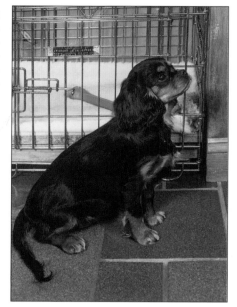

Place the crate in a quiet place in the home, not too far from where the family gathers. Your Cavalier will look forward to resting in his crate once he tires from his day of business.

house again. Never hit a puppy or put his face in urine or excrement when he has an accident!

Once indoors, put the puppy in his crate until you have time to clean up his accident. Then release him to the family area and watch him more closely than before. Chances are, his accident was a result of your not picking up his signal or waiting too long before offering him the opportunity to relieve himself. Never hold a grudge against the puppy for accidents.

Let the puppy learn that going outdoors means it is time to relieve himself, not play. Once trained, he will be able to play indoors and out and still differentiate between the times for play versus the times for relief.

Help him develop regular hours for naps, being alone, playing by himself and just resting, all in his crate. Encourage him to entertain himself while you are busy with your activities. Let him learn that having you near is comforting, but it is not your main purpose in life to provide him with undivided attention. Each time you put a puppy in his own area, use the same command, whatever suits best. Soon, he will run to his crate or special area when he hears you say those words. Crate training provides safety for you, the puppy and the home. It also provides the puppy with a feeling of security, and that helps the puppy achieve self-confidence and clean habits.

Remember that one of the primary ingredients in house-training your puppy is control. Regardless of your lifestyle, there will always be occasions when you will need to have a place where your dog can stay and be happy and safe. Crate training is

TAKE THE LEAD
Do not carry your dog to his relief area. Lead him there on a leash or, better yet, encourage him to follow you to the spot. If you start carrying him to his spot, you might end up doing this routine forever and your dog will have the satisfaction of having trained *you*.

THE SUCCESS METHOD

Success that comes by luck is usually short-lived. Success that comes by well-thought-out proven methods is often more easily achieved and permanent. This is the Success Method. It is designed to give you, the puppy owner, a simple yet proven way to help your puppy develop clean living habits and a feeling of security in his new environment.

6 Steps to Successful Crate Training

1 Tell the puppy "Crate time!" and place him in the crate with a small treat (a piece of cheese or half of a biscuit). Let him stay in the crate for five minutes while you are in the same room. Then release him and praise lavishly. Never release him when he is fussing. Wait until he is quiet before you let him out.

2 Repeat Step 1 several times a day.

3 The next day, place the puppy in the crate as before. Let him stay there for ten minutes. Do this several times.

4 Continue building time in five-minute increments until the puppy stays in his crate for 30 minutes with you in the room. Always take him to his relief area after prolonged periods in his crate.

5 Now go back to Step 1 and let the puppy stay in his crate for five minutes, this time while you are out of the room.

6 Once again, build crate time in five-minute increments with you out of the room. When the puppy will stay willingly in his crate (he may even fall asleep!) for 30 minutes with you out of the room, he will be ready to stay in it for several hours at a time.

HOW MANY TIMES A DAY?

AGE	RELIEF TRIPS
To 14 weeks	10
14–22 weeks	8
22–32 weeks	6
Adulthood	4
(dog stops growing)	

These are estimates, of course, but they are a guide to the minimum number of opportunities a dog should have each day to relieve himself.

the answer for now and in the future.

In conclusion, a few key elements are really all you need for a successful house-training method—consistency, frequency, praise, control and supervision. By following these procedures with a normal, healthy puppy, you and the puppy will soon be past the stage of "accidents" and ready to move on to a clean and rewarding life together.

Your Cavalier puppy is easily trained to know that going outside means relief time.

ROLES OF DISCIPLINE, REWARD AND PUNISHMENT

Discipline, training one to act in accordance with rules, brings order to life. It is as simple as that. Without discipline, particularly in a group society, chaos reigns supreme and the group will eventually perish. Humans and canines are social animals and need some form of discipline in order to function effectively. They must procure food, protect their home base and reproduce to keep the species going. If there were no discipline in the lives of social animals, they would eventually die from starvation and/or predation by other stronger animals.

In the case of domestic canines, dogs need discipline in their lives in order to understand how their pack (you and other family members) functions and how they must act in order to survive.

A large humane society in a highly populated area recently surveyed dog owners regarding their satisfaction with their relationships with their dogs. People who had trained their dogs were 75% more satisfied with their pets than those who had never trained their dogs.

Dr. Edward Thorndike, a noted psychologist, established *Thorndike's Theory of Learning*, which states that a behavior that results in a pleasant event tends to be repeated. A behavior that results in an unpleasant event, therefore, tends not to be repeated. It is this theory on which training methods are based

CALM DOWN

Dogs will do anything for your attention. If you reward the dog when he is calm and attentive, you will develop a well-mannered dog. If, on the other hand, you greet your dog excitedly and encourage him to wrestle with you, the dog will greet you the same way and you will have a hyperactive dog on your hands.

today. For example, if you manipulate a dog to perform a specific behavior and reward him for doing it, he is likely to do it again because he enjoyed the end result.

Occasionally, punishment, a penalty inflicted for an offense, is necessary. The best type of punishment often comes from an outside source. For example, a child is told not to touch the stove because he may get burned. He disobeys and touches the stove. In doing so, he receives a burn. From

that time on, he respects the heat of the stove and avoids contact with it. Therefore, a behavior that results in an unpleasant event tends not to be repeated.

A good example of a dog learning the hard way is the dog who chases the house cat. He is told many times to leave the cat alone, yet he persists in teasing the cat. Then, one day he begins chasing the cat but the cat turns and swipes a claw across the dog's face, leaving him with a painful gash on his nose. The final result is that the dog stops chasing the cat.

Be careful never to leave your Cavalier crated while outdoors in the sun. A dog can suffer heatstroke quite readily so an owner must be very cautious.

You should make a habit of cleaning up your dog's droppings wherever they may be. Handy sanitation devices are available at most pet shops.

Leash training will be your Cavalier's first taste of obedience. He should accept the leash in no time and look forward to outings with his owner.

TRAINING EQUIPMENT

COLLAR AND LEAD

For a Cavalier the collar and lead that you use for training must be one with which you are easily able to work, not too heavy for the dog and perfectly safe.

TREATS

Have a bag of treats on hand. Something nutritious and easy to swallow works best. Use a soft treat, a chunk of cheese or a piece of cooked chicken rather than a dry biscuit. By the time the dog gets done chewing a dry treat, he will forget why he is being rewarded in the first place! In training, rewarding the dog with a food treat will help him associate praise and the treats with learning

new behaviors that obviously please his owner. Using food rewards will not teach a dog to beg at the table—the only way to teach a dog to beg at the table is to give him food from the table.

TRAINING BEGINS: ASK THE DOG A QUESTION

In order to teach your dog anything, you must first get his attention. After all, he cannot learn anything if he is looking away from you with his mind on something else.

To get his attention, ask him "School?" and immediately walk over to him and give him a treat

PLAN TO PLAY

The puppy should also have regular play and exercise sessions when he is with you or a family member. Exercise for a very young puppy can consist of a short walk around the house or yard. Playing can include fetching games with a large ball or a special toy. (All puppies teethe and need soft things upon which to chew.) Remember to restrict play periods to indoors within his living area (the family room, for example) until he is completely house-trained.

as you tell him "Good dog." Wait a minute or two and repeat the routine, this time with a treat in your hand as you approach within a foot of the dog. Do not go directly to him, but stop about a foot short of him and hold out the treat as you ask "School?" He will see you approaching with a treat in your hand and most likely begin walking toward you. As you meet, give him the treat and praise again.

The third time, ask the question, have a treat in your hand and walk only a short distance toward the dog so that he must walk almost all the way to you. As he reaches you, give him the treat and praise again.

By this time, the dog will probably be getting the idea that if he pays attention to you, especially when you ask that question, it will pay off in treats and fun activities for him. In other words, he learns that "school" means

doing fun things with you that result in treats and positive attention for him.

Remember that the dog does not understand your verbal language, he only recognizes sounds. Your question translates to a series of sounds for him, and those sounds become the signal to go to you and pay attention; if he does, he will get to interact with you plus receive treats and praise.

Offer your puppy small treats for correct behavior. Be careful not to overfeed the puppy during his training sessions or else he'll regard "school" as another mealtime.

THE BASIC COMMANDS

TEACHING SIT

Now that you have the dog's attention, attach his lead and hold it in your left hand and a food treat in your right. Place your food hand at the dog's nose and let him lick the treat but not take it from you. Say "Sit" and slowly raise your food hand from in front of the dog's nose up over his head so that he is looking at the ceiling. As he bends his head upward, he will have to bend his knees to

---

TRAINING RULES

If you want to be successful in training your dog, you have four rules to obey yourself:

1. Develop an understanding of how a dog thinks.
2. Do not blame the dog for lack of communication.
3. Define your dog's personality and act accordingly.
4. Have patience and be consistent.

Training your Cavalier to sit is an easy task. Use the food treat to keep the dog's attention.

maintain his balance. As he bends his knees, he will assume a sit position. At that point, release the food treat and praise lavishly with comments such as "Good dog! Good sit!" Remember to always praise enthusiastically, because dogs relish verbal praise from their owners and feel so proud of themselves whenever they accomplish a behavior.

You will not use food forever in getting the dog to obey your commands. Food is only used to teach new behaviors, and once the dog knows what you want when you give a specific command, you will wean him off the food treats but still maintain the verbal praise. After all, you will always have your voice with you, and there will be many times when

you have no food rewards but expect the dog to obey.

TEACHING DOWN

Teaching the down exercise is easy when you understand how the dog perceives the down position, and it is very difficult when you do not. Dogs perceive the down position as a submissive one, therefore teaching the down exercise using a forceful method can sometimes make the dog develop such a fear of the down that he either runs away when you say "Down" or he attempts to snap at the person who tries to force him down.

Have the dog sit close alongside your left leg, facing in the same direction as you are. Hold the lead in your left hand and a food treat in your right. Now

---

LANGUAGE BARRIER

Dogs do not understand our language and have to rely on tone of voice more than just words or sound. They can be trained to react to a certain sound, at a certain volume. If you say "No, Oliver" in a very soft, pleasant voice, it will not have the same meaning as "No, Oliver!!" when you raise your voice.

You should never use the dog's name during a reprimand, just the command "No! " You never want the dog to associate his name with a negative experience or reprimand.

place your left hand lightly on the top of the dog's shoulders where they meet above the spinal cord. Do not push down on the dog's shoulders; simply rest your left hand there so you can guide the dog to lie down close to your left leg rather than to swing away from your side when he drops.

Now place the food hand at the dog's nose, say "Down" very softly (almost a whisper), and slowly lower the food hand to the dog's front feet. When the food hand reaches the floor, begin moving it forward along the floor in front of the dog. Keep talking softly to the dog, saying things like, "Do you want this treat? You can do this, good dog." Your reassuring tone of voice will help calm the dog as he tries to follow the food hand in order to get the treat.

When the dog's elbows touch the floor, release the food and praise softly. Try to get the dog to maintain that down position for several seconds before you let him sit up again. The goal here is to get your Cavalier to settle down and not feel threatened in the down position.

TEACHING STAY

It is easy to teach the dog to stay in either a sit or a down position. Again, we use food and praise during the teaching process as we help the dog to understand exactly what it is that we are expecting him to do.

Once your Cavalier has learned to obey your sit command, start to move away from him slowly repeating the sit command. This is the beginning of the stay.

To teach the sit/stay, start with the dog sitting on your left side as before and hold the lead in your left hand. Have a food treat in your right hand and place your food hand at the dog's nose. Say "Stay" and step out on your right foot to stand directly in front of the dog, toe to toe, as he licks and

DOUBLE JEOPARDY

A dog in jeopardy never lies down. He stays alert on his feet because instinct tells him that he may have to run away or fight for his survival. Therefore, if a dog feels threatened or anxious, he will not lie down. Consequently, it is important to keep the dog calm and relaxed as he learns the down exercise.

nibbles the treat. Be sure to keep his head facing upward to maintain the sit position. Count to five and then swing around to stand next to the dog again with him on your left. As soon as you get back

The down position is not a natural one for dogs. In their own world, dogs lie down in fear or submission, and in repose. Using a gentle approach (and a tasty morsel), you can convince your Cav that down is a good place to be.

to the original position, release the food and praise lavishly.

To teach the down/stay, do the down as previously described. As soon as the dog lies down, say "Stay" and step out on your right foot just as you did in the sit/stay. Count to five and then return to stand beside the dog with him on your left side. Release the treat and praise as always.

Within a week or ten days, you can begin to add a bit of distance between you and your dog when you leave him. When you do, use your left hand open with the palm facing the dog as a stay signal, much the same as the hand signal a police officer uses to stop traffic at an intersection. Hold the food treat in your right hand as before, but this time the food is not touching

the dog's nose. He will watch the food hand and quickly learn that he is going to get that treat as soon as you return to his side.

When you can stand 3 feet away from your dog for 30 seconds, you can then begin building time and distance in both stays. Eventually, the dog can be expected to remain in the stay position for prolonged periods of time until you return to him or call him to you. Always praise when he stays.

TEACHING COME

If you make teaching the come a fun experience, you should never have a student that does not love the game or that fails to come when called. The secret, it seems, is never to teach the word "come."

At times when an owner most wants his dog to come when called, the owner is likely upset or anxious and he allows these feelings to come through in the tone of his voice when he calls his dog. Hearing that desperation in his owner's voice, the dog fears the results of going to him and therefore either disobeys outright or runs in the opposite direction. The secret, therefore, is to teach the dog a game and, when you want him to come to you, simply play the game. It is practically a no-fail solution!

To begin, have several members of your family take a few

food treats and each go into a different room in the house. Take turns calling the dog, and each person should celebrate the dog's finding him with a treat and lots of happy praise. When a person calls the dog, he is actually inviting the dog to find him and get a treat as a reward for "winning."

A few turns of the "Where are you?" game and the dog will figure out that everyone is playing the game and that each person has a big celebration awaiting his success at locating them. Once he

"WHERE ARE YOU?"

When calling the dog, do not say "Come." Say things like, 'Rover, where are you? See if you can find me! I have a biscuit for you!" Keep up a constant line of chatter with coaxing sounds and frequent questions such as, "Where are you?" The dog will learn to follow the sound of your voice to locate you and receive his reward.

learns to love the game, simply calling out "Where are you?" will bring him running from wherever he is when he hears that all-important question.

The come command is recognized as one of the most important things to teach a dog, but there are trainers who work with thousands of dogs and never teach the actual word "come." Yet these dogs will race to respond to a

person who uses the dog's name followed by "Where are you?" For example, a woman has a 12-year-old companion dog who went blind, but who never fails to locate her owner when asked, "Where are you?"

Children particularly love to play this game with their dogs. Children can hide in smaller places like a shower stall or bathtub, behind a bed or under a table. The dog needs to work a little bit harder to find these hiding places, but when he does he loves to celebrate with a treat and a tussle with a favorite youngster.

TEACHING HEEL

Heeling means that the dog walks beside the owner without pulling. It takes time and patience on the owner's part to succeed at teaching the dog that he (the owner)

Always speak in a happy tone of voice when calling your Cavalier to you. If he senses that you're anxious or angry, he will hesitate to come near you.

you in what we now call the heel position. Praise verbally, but do not touch the dog. Hesitate a moment and begin again with "Heel," taking three steps and stopping, at which point the dog is told to sit again.

Your goal here is to have the dog walk those three steps without pulling on the lead. When he will walk calmly beside you for three steps without pulling, increase the number of steps you take to five. When he will walk politely beside you while you take five steps, you can increase the length of your walk to ten steps. Keep increasing the length of your stroll until the dog will walk quietly beside you without pulling as long as you want him to heel. When you stop heeling, indicate to the dog that the exercise is over by verbally praising as you pet him and say "OK, good dog." The "OK" is used as a release word, meaning that the exercise is finished and the dog is free to relax.

If you are dealing with a dog who insists on pulling you

Adult Cavs, just like their puppy counterparts, revel in positive reinforcement from their masters. Tell him, "Good dog" every time he obeys your command.

will not proceed unless the dog is walking calmly beside him. Pulling out ahead on the lead is definitely not acceptable.

Begin with holding the lead in your left hand as the dog sits beside your left leg. Move the loop end of the lead to your right hand but keep your left hand short on the lead so it keeps the dog in close next to you.

Say "Heel" and step forward on your left foot. Keep the dog close to you and take three steps. Stop and have the dog sit next to

HEELING WELL

Teach your dog to heel in an enclosed area. Once you think the dog will obey reliably and you want to attempt advanced obedience exercises such as off-lead heeling, test him in a fenced-in area so he cannot run away.

around, simply "put on your brakes" and stand your ground until the dog realizes that the two of you are not going anywhere until he is beside you and moving at your pace, not his. It may take some time just standing there to convince the dog that you are the leader and you will be the one to decide on the direction and speed of your travel.

Each time the dog looks up at you or slows down to give a slack lead between the two of you, quietly praise him and say, "Good heel. Good dog." Eventually, the dog will begin to respond and within a few days he will be walking politely beside you without pulling on the lead. At first, the training sessions should be kept short and very positive; soon the dog will be able to walk nicely with you for increasingly longer distances. Remember also to give the dog free time and the opportunity to run and play when you are done with heel practice.

Teaching your dog to 'Heel' begins with the dog in a sitting position. Cavaliers are easy to train because they are so intelligent and eager to please.

TUG OF WALK?
If you begin teaching the heel by taking long walks and letting the dog pull you along, he misinterprets this action as an acceptable form of taking a walk. When you pull back on the leash to counteract his pulling, he reads that tug as a signal to pull even harder!

WEANING OFF FOOD IN TRAINING
Food is used in training new behaviors. Once the dog understands what behavior goes with a specific command, it is time to start weaning him off the food treats. At first, give a treat after each exercise. Then, start to give a treat only after every other exer-

cise. Mix up the times when you offer a food reward and the times when you only offer praise so that the dog will never know when he is going to receive both food and praise and when he is going to receive only praise. This is called a variable-ratio reward system and it proves successful because there is always the chance that the owner will produce a treat, so the dog never stops trying for that reward. No matter what, *always* give verbal praise.

OBEDIENCE CLASSES
It is a good idea to enroll in an obedience class if one is available in your area. If yours is a show

Cavaliers love to accompany their owners on any number of outings, from dog shows to obedience classes to family picnics.

dog, conformation training classes would be more appropriate. Many areas have dog clubs that offer basic obedience training as well as preparatory classes for obedience competition. There are also local dog trainers who offer similar classes.

FAMILY TIES
If you have other pets in the home and/or interact often with the pets of friends and other family members, your pup will respond to those pets in much the same manner as you do. It is only when you show fear of or resentment toward another animal that he will act fearful or unfriendly.

OTHER ACTIVITIES FOR LIFE
Whether a dog is trained in the structured environment of a class or alone with his owner at home, there are many activities that can bring fun and rewards to both owner and dog once they have mastered basic control.

Teaching the dog to help out around the home, in the yard or on the farm provides great satisfaction to both dog and owner. In addition, the dog's help makes life a little easier for his owner and raises his stature as a valued companion to his family. It helps give the dog a purpose by occupying his mind and providing an outlet for his energy.

Hiking is an exciting and healthy activity that the dog can be taught without assistance from more than his owner. The exercise of walking and climbing is good for man and dog alike, and the bond that they develop together is priceless. For the sporting enthusiast, the Cavalier is happy to participate in a weekend hunting excursion. He is a spaniel after all!

At obedience trials, dogs can earn titles at various levels of competition. The beginning levels of competition include basic exercises like sit, down, heel, etc. The more advanced levels of competition include jumping, retrieving,

scent discrimination and signal work. The advanced levels require a dog and owner to put a lot of time and effort into their training and the titles that can be earned at these levels of competition are very prestigious.

If you are interested in participating in organized competition with your Cavalier, there are activities other than obedience in which you and your dog can become involved. Agility is a popular and fun sport where dogs run through an obstacle course that includes various jumps, tunnels and other exercises to test the dog's speed and coordination. The owners run through the course beside their dogs to give commands and to guide them through the course. Although competitive, the focus is on fun—it's fun to do, it's fun to watch and it's great exercise

Although most people think of the Cavalier as an indoor house pet, let's not forget the "Spaniel" in his name. Cavs can be trained to work in the field, just like their larger Cocker and Springer relations.

PRACTICE MAKES PERFECT!

- Have training lessons with your dog every day in several short segments—three to five times a day for a few minutes at a time is ideal.
- Do not have long practice sessions. The dog will become easily bored.
- Never practice when you are tired, ill, worried or in an otherwise negative mood. This will transmit to the dog and may have an adverse effect on his performance.

  Think fun, short and above all *positive!* End each session on a high note, rather than a failed exercise, and make sure to give a lot of praise. Enjoy the training and help your dog enjoy it, too.

Internal Organs with Skeletal Structure

1. Esophagus
2. Lungs
3. Gall Bladder
4. Liver
5. Kidney
6. Stomach
7. Intestines
8. Urinary Bladder

CAVALIER KING CHARLES SPANIEL

Dogs suffer from many of the same physical illnesses as people. They might even share many of the same psychological problems. Since people usually know more about human diseases than canine maladies, many of the terms used in this chapter will be familiar but not necessarily those used by veterinarians. We will use the term *x-ray*, instead of the more acceptable term *radiograph*. We will also use the familiar term *symptoms* even though dogs don't have symptoms, which are verbal descriptions of the patient's feelings: dogs have clinical signs. Since dogs can't speak, we have to look for clinical signs...but we still use the term *symptoms* in this book.

As a general rule, medicine is practiced. That term is not arbitrary. Medicine is a constantly changing art as we learn more and more about genetics, electronic aids (like CAT scans and MRIs) and daily laboratory advances. There are many dog maladies, like canine hip dysplasia, which are not universally treated in the same manner. Some veterinarians opt for surgery more often than others do.

SELECTING A VETERINARIAN

Your selection of a veterinarian should be based not only upon personality and ability with dogs but also upon his convenience to

Select a vet convenient to your home. Don't be hesitant to discuss fees, office hours, policies, etc., before deciding on a vet.

your home. You want a vet who is close because you might have emergencies or need to make multiple visits for treatments. You want a vet who has services that you might require such as a boarding kennel and grooming facilities, as well as pet supplies and a good reputation for ability and responsiveness. There is nothing more frustrating than having to wait a day or more to

Breakdown of Veterinary Income by Category

2%	Dentistry
4%	Radiology
12%	Surgery
15%	Vaccinations
19%	Laboratory
23%	Examinations
25%	Medicines

A typical vet's income, categorized according to services performed. This survey dealt with small-animal (pets) practices.

get a response from your veterinarian.

All veterinarians are licensed and their diplomas and/or certificates should be displayed in their waiting rooms. There are, however, many veterinary specialties that usually require further studies and internships. There are specialists in heart problems (veterinary cardiologists), skin problems (veterinary dermatologists), teeth and gum problems (veterinary dentists), eye problems (veterinary ophthalmologists), x-rays (veterinary radiologists), and vets who have specialties in bones, muscles or certain organs. Most veterinarians do routine surgery such as neutering, stitching up wounds and docking tails for those breeds in which such is required for show purposes. When the problem affecting your dog is

serious, it is not unusual or impudent to get another medical opinion, although it is courteous are obliged to advise the vets concerned about this. You might also want to compare costs among several veterinarians. Sophisticated health care and veterinary services can be very costly. Don't be bashful about discussing these costs with your veterinarian or his staff. It is not infrequent that important decisions are based upon financial considerations.

PREVENTATIVE MEDICINE
It is much easier, less costly and more effective to practice preventative medicine than to fight bouts of illness and disease. Properly bred puppies come from parents that were selected based upon their genetic-disease profiles. Their dam should have been vaccinated, free of all internal and external parasites, and properly nourished. For these reasons, a visit to the veterinarian who cared for the dam (mother) is recommended. The dam can pass on disease resistance to her puppies, which can last for eight to ten weeks. She can also pass on parasites and many infections. It's a good idea to learn as much about the dam's health as you can.

WEANING TO FIVE MONTHS OLD
Puppies should be weaned by the time they are about two months

First Aid at a Glance

Burns
Place the affected area under cool water; use ice if only a small area is burnt.

Bee stings/Insect bites
Apply ice to relieve swelling; antihistamine dosed properly.

Animal bites
Clean any bleeding area; apply pressure until bleeding subsides; go to the vet.

Spider bites
Use cold compress and a pressurized pack to inhibit venom's spreading.

Antifreeze poisoning
Induce vomiting with hydrogen peroxide. Seek *immediate* veterinary help!

Fish hooks
Removal best handled by vet; hook must be cut in order to remove.

Snake bites
Pack ice around bite; contact vet quickly; identify snake for proper antivenin.

Car accident
Move dog from roadway with blanket; seek veterinary aid.

Shock
Calm the dog; keep him warm; seek immediate veterinary help.

Nosebleed
Apply cold compress to the nose; apply pressure to any visible abrasion.

Bleeding
Apply pressure above the area; treat wound by applying a cotton pack.

Heat stroke
Submerge dog in cold bath; cool down with fresh air and water; go to the vet.

Frostbite/Hypothermia
Warm the dog with a warm bath, electric blankets or hot water bottles.

Abrasions
Clean the wound and wash out thoroughly with fresh water; apply antiseptic.

!! *Remember: an injured dog may attempt to bite a helping hand from fear and confusion. Always muzzle the dog before trying to offer assistance.* **!!**

Discuss your Cavalier's inoculation schedule with your veterinarian. Keep track of every injection that your dog receives.

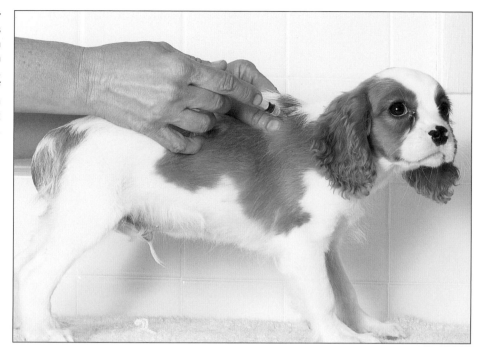

old. A puppy that remains for at least eight weeks with his dam and littermates usually adapts better to other dogs and people later in life.

Some new owners have their puppy examined by a veterinarian immediately, which is a good idea. Vaccination programs usually begin when the puppy is very young. The puppy will have his teeth examined and have his skeletal conformation and general health checked prior to certification by the veterinarian. Puppies in certain breeds have problems with their kneecaps, cataracts and other eye problems, heart murmurs and undescended testi-cles. They may also have personality problems and your veterinarian might have training in temperament evaluation.

PUPPY VACCINATIONS

Your veterinarian will probably recommend that your puppy be fully vaccinated before you take him outside. There are airborne diseases, parasite eggs in the grass and unexpected visits from other dogs that might be dangerous to your puppy's health. Other dogs are the most harmful reservoir of pathogenic organisms, as everything they have can be transmitted to your puppy.

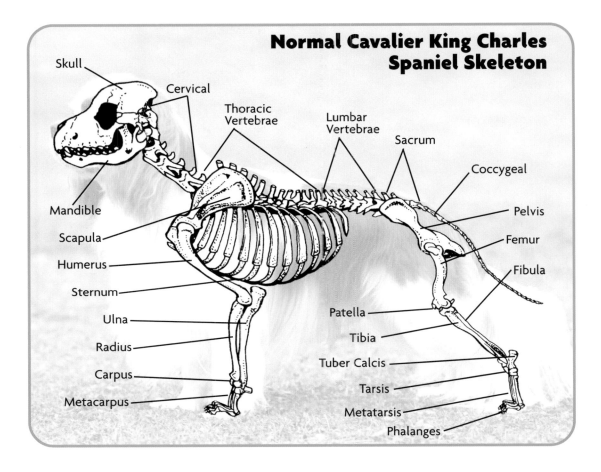

Normal Cavalier King Charles Spaniel Skeleton

Skull
Cervical
Thoracic Vertebrae
Lumbar Vertebrae
Sacrum
Coccygeal
Mandible
Pelvis
Scapula
Femur
Humerus
Fibula
Sternum
Patella
Ulna
Tibia
Radius
Tuber Calcis
Carpus
Tarsis
Metacarpus
Metatarsis
Phalanges

Vaccination Scheduling

Most vaccinations are given by injection and should only be done by a veterinarian. Both he and you should keep a record of the date of the injection, the identification of the vaccine and the amount given. Some vets give a first vaccination at eight weeks, but most dog breeders prefer the course not to commence until about ten weeks because of negating any antibodies passed on by the dam. The vaccination scheduling is usually based on a 15-day cycle. You must take your vet's advice as to when to vaccinate as this may differ according to the vaccine used. Most vaccinations immunize your puppy against viruses.

The usual vaccines contain immunizing doses of several

HEALTH AND VACCINATION SCHEDULE

Age in Weeks:	6th	8th	10th	12th	14th	16th	20-24th	52nd
Worm Control	✔	✔	✔	✔	✔	✔	✔	
Neutering							✔	
Heartworm		✔		✔		✔	✔	
Parvovirus	✔		✔		✔		✔	✔
Distemper		✔		✔		✔		✔
Hepatitis		✔		✔		✔		✔
Leptospirosis								✔
Parainfluenza	✔		✔		✔			✔
Dental Examination		✔					✔	✔
Complete Physical		✔					✔	✔
Coronavirus				✔			✔	✔
Canine Cough	✔							
Hip Dysplasia								✔
Rabies							✔	

Vaccinations are not instantly effective. It takes about two weeks for the dog's immune system to develop antibodies. Most vaccinations require annual booster shots. Your vet should guide you in this regard.

different viruses such as distemper, parvovirus, parainfluenza and hepatitis. There are other vaccines available when the puppy is at risk. You should rely upon professional advice. This is especially true for the booster-shot program. Most vaccination programs require a booster when the puppy is a year old and once a year thereafter. In some cases, circumstances may require more frequent immunizations. Canine cough, more formally known as tracheobronchitis, is treated with a vaccine that is sprayed into the dog's nostrils. Canine cough is usually included in routine vaccination, but this is often not so effective as for other major diseases.

VACCINE ALLERGIES

Vaccines do not work all the time. Sometimes dogs are allergic to them and many times the antibodies, which are supposed to be stimulated by the vaccine, just are not produced. You should keep your dog in the veterinary clinic for an hour after it is vaccinated to be sure there are no allergic reactions.

FIVE MONTHS TO ONE YEAR OF AGE
Unless you intend to breed or show your dog, neutering the puppy at six months of age is recommended. Discuss this with your vet.

By the time your Cavalier King Charles Spaniel is seven or eight months of age, he can be seriously evaluated for his conformation to the standard, thus determining show potential and desirability as a sire or dam. If the puppy is not top class and therefore is not a candidate for a serious breeding program, most professionals advise neutering the puppy. Neutering and spaying have proven to be extremely beneficial to both male and female puppies, respectively. Besides eliminating the possibility of pregnancy, it inhibits (but does not prevent) pyometra and breast cancer in bitches and testicular cancer and prostate cancer in male dogs. Under no circumstances should a bitch be spayed prior to her first season.

DOGS OLDER THAN ONE YEAR
Continue to visit the veterinarian at least once a year. There is no such disease as old age, but

DISEASE REFERENCE CHART

	What is it?	What causes it?	Symptoms
Leptospirosis	Severe disease that affects the internal organs; can be spread to people.	A bacterium, which is often carried by rodents, that enters through mucous membranes and spreads quickly throughout the body.	Range from fever, vomiting and loss of appetite in less severe cases to shock, irreversible kidney damage and possibly death in most severe cases.
Rabies	Potentially deadly virus that infects warm-blooded mammals.	Bite from a carrier of the virus, mainly wild animals.	1st stage: dog exhibits change in behavior, fear. 2nd stage: dog's behavior becomes more aggressive. 3rd stage: loss of coordination, trouble with bodily functions.
Parvovirus	Highly contagious virus, potentially deadly.	Ingestion of the virus, which is usually spread through the feces of infected dogs.	Most common: severe diarrhea. Also vomiting, fatigue, lack of appetite.
Canine cough	Contagious respiratory infection.	Combination of types of bacteria and virus. Most common: *Bordetella bronchiseptica* bacteria and parainfluenza virus.	Chronic cough.
Distemper	Disease primarily affecting respiratory and nervous system.	Virus that is related to the human measles virus.	Mild symptoms such as fever, lack of appetite and mucus secretion progress to evidence of brain damage, "hard pad."
Hepatitis	Virus primarily affecting the liver.	Canine adenovirus type I (CAV-1). Enters system when dog breathes in particles.	Lesser symptoms include listlessness, diarrhea, vomiting. More severe symptoms include "blue-eye" (clumps of virus in eye).
Coronavirus	Virus resulting in digestive problems.	Virus is spread through infected dog's feces.	Stomach upset evidenced by lack of appetite, vomiting, diarrhea.

DENTAL HEALTH

A dental examination is in order when the dog is between six months and one year of age so that any permanent teeth that have erupted incorrectly can be corrected. It is important to begin a brushing routine at home, using dental-care products made for dogs, such as special toothbrushes and toothpaste. Durable nylon and safe edible chews should be a part of your puppy's arsenal for good health, good teeth and pleasant breath. The vast majority of dogs three to four years old and older has diseases of the gums from lack of dental attention. Using the various types of dental chews can be very effective in controlling dental plaque.

bodily functions do change with age. The eyes and ears are no longer as efficient. Liver, kidney and intestinal functions often decline. Proper dietary changes, recommended by your veterinarian, can make life more pleasant for the aging Cavalier King Charles Spaniel.

SKIN PROBLEMS IN CAVALIER KING CHARLES SPANIELS

Veterinarians are consulted by dog owners for skin problems more than for any other group of diseases or maladies. Dogs' skin is almost as sensitive as human skin and both suffer almost the same ailments, though the occurrence of acne in dogs is rare! For this reason, veterinary dermatology has developed into a specialty practiced by many veterinarians.

Since many skin problems have visual symptoms that are almost identical, it requires the skill of an experienced veterinary dermatologist to identify and cure many of the more severe skin disorders. Pet shops sell many treatments for skin problems but most of the treatments are directed at symptoms and not the underlying problem(s). If your dog is suffering from a skin disorder, you should seek professional assistance as quickly as possible. As with all diseases, the earlier a problem is identified and treated, the more successful can be the cure.

HEREDITARY SKIN DISORDERS

Veterinary dermatologists are currently researching a number of skin disorders that are believed to have hereditary bases. These inherited diseases are transmitted by both parents, who appear (phenotypically) normal but have a recessive gene for the disease, meaning that they carry, but are not affected by, the disease. These diseases pose serious problems to breeders because in some instances there are no methods of identifying carriers, although the occurrence of these diseases in

Cavaliers is not too common. Sometimes the secondary diseases associated with these skin conditions are even more debilitating than the skin disorders themselves, including cancers and respiratory problems.

Among the hereditary skin disorders, for which the mode of inheritance is known, are acrodermatitis, cutaneous asthenia (Ehlers-Danlos syndrome), sebaceous adenitis, cyclic hematopoiesis, dermatomyositis, IgA deficiency, color dilution alopecia and nodular dermatofibrosis. Some of these disorders are limited to one or two breeds, while others affect a large number of breeds. If you detect any growths or other abnormalities on your Cavalier's skin, report it to your veterinarian immediately. All inherited diseases must be diagnosed and treated by a veterinary specialist.

PARASITE BITES

Many of us are allergic to insect bites. The bites itch, erupt and may even become infected. Dogs have the same reaction to fleas, ticks and/or mites. When an insect lands on you, you have the chance to whisk it away with your hand. Unfortunately, when your dog is bitten by a flea, tick or mite, it can only scratch it away or bite it. By the time the dog has been bitten, the parasite has done some of its damage. It may also have laid eggs to cause further problems in the near future. The itching from parasite bites is probably due to the saliva injected into the site when the parasite sucks the dog's blood.

AUTO-IMMUNE SKIN CONDITIONS

Auto-immune skin conditions are commonly referred to as being allergic to yourself, while allergies are usually inflammatory reactions to an outside stimulus. Auto-immune diseases cause serious damage to the tissues that are involved.

The best known auto-immune disease is lupus, which affects people as well as dogs. The symptoms are variable and may affect the kidneys bones, blood chemistry and skin. It can be fatal to both dogs and humans, though it is not thought to be transmissible. It is usually successfully treated with cortisone, prednisone or a

NEUTERING/SPAYING

Male dogs are castrated. The operation removes both testicles and requires that the dog be anesthetized. Recovery takes about one week. Females are spayed; in this operation, the uterus (womb) and both of the ovaries are removed. This is major surgery, also carried out under general anesthesia, and it usually takes a bitch two weeks to recover.

similar corticosteroid, but extensive use of these drugs can have harmful side effects.

AIRBORNE ALLERGIES

Just as humans have hay fever, rose fever and other fevers from which they suffer during the pollinating season, many dogs suffer from the same allergies. When the pollen count is high, your dog might suffer but don't expect him to sneeze and have a runny nose as a human would. Dogs react to pollen allergies the same way they react to fleas—they scratch and bite themselves.

A SKUNKY PROBLEM

Have you noticed your dog dragging his rump along the floor? If so, it is likely that his anal sacs are impacted or possibly infected. The anal sacs are small pouches located on both sides of the anus under the skin and muscles. They are about the size and shape of a grape and contain a foul-smelling liquid. Their contents are usually emptied when the dog has a bowel movement but, if not emptied completely, they will impact, which will cause your dog much pain. Fortunately, your veterinarian can tend to this problem easily by draining the sacs for the dog. Be aware that your dog might also empty his anal sacs in cases of extreme fright.

Dogs, like humans, can be tested for allergens. Discuss the testing with your veterinary dermatologist.

FOOD PROBLEMS

FOOD ALLERGIES

Dogs are allergic to many foods that are best-sellers and highly recommended by breeders and veterinarians. Changing the brand of food that you buy may not eliminate the problem if the element to which the dog is allergic is contained in the new brand.

Recognizing a food allergy is difficult. Humans vomit or have rashes when we eat a food to which we are allergic. Dogs neither vomit nor (usually) develop a rash. They react in the same manner as they do to an airborne or flea allergy: they itch, scratch and bite. This makes the diagnosis extremely difficult. While pollen allergies and parasite bites are usually seasonal, food allergies are year-round problems.

FOOD INTOLERANCE

Food intolerance is the inability of the dog to completely digest certain foods. For example, puppies that may have done very well on their mother's milk may not do well on cow's milk. The result of this food intolerance may be loose bowels, passing gas and stomach pains. These are the only obvious symptoms of food intolerance and that makes diagnosis difficult.

TREATING FOOD PROBLEMS

It is possible to handle food allergies and food intolerance yourself. Put your dog on a diet that he has never had. Obviously if he has never eaten this new food he can't have been allergic or intolerant of it. Start with a single ingredient that is not in the dog's diet at the present time. Ingredients like chopped beef or chicken are common in dog's diets, so try something different like lamb or fish. Keep the dog on this diet (with no additives) for a month. If the symptoms of food allergy or intolerance disappear, chances are your dog has a food allergy.

Don't think that the single ingredient cured the problem. You still must find a suitable diet and ascertain which ingredient in the old diet was objectionable. This is most easily done by adding ingredients to the new diet one at a time. Let the dog stay on the modified diet for a month before you add another ingredient. Eventually, you will determine the ingredient that caused the adverse reaction.

An alternative method is to carefully study the ingredients in the diet to which your dog is allergic or intolerable. Identify the main ingredient in this diet and eliminate the main ingredient by buying a different food that does not have that ingredient. Keep experimenting until the symptoms disappear after one month on the new diet.

The pollen in flowers may cause an allergic reaction. If your dog has an allergy of any kind, as indicated by constant scratching, report this to your vet.

A male dog flea, *Ctenocephalides canis.*

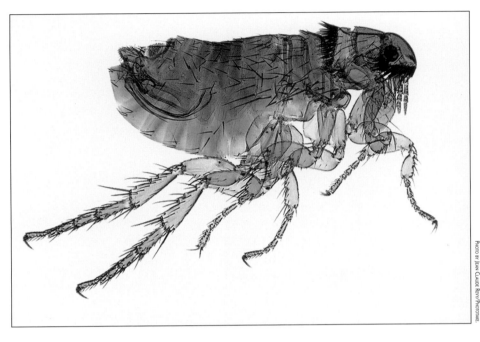

PHOTO BY JEAN CLAUDE REVY/PHOTOTAKE.

EXTERNAL PARASITES

FLEAS

Of all the problems to which dogs are prone, none is more well known and frustrating than fleas. Flea infestation is relatively simple to cure but difficult to prevent. Parasites that are harbored inside the body are a bit more difficult to eradicate but they are easier to control.

To control flea infestation, you have to understand the flea's life cycle. Fleas are often thought of as a summertime problem, but centrally heated homes have changed the patterns and fleas can be found at any time of the year. The most effective method of flea control is a two-stage approach: one stage to kill the adult fleas, and the other to control the development of pre-adult fleas. Unfortunately, no single active ingredient is effective against all stages of the life cycle.

FLEA KILLER CAUTION— "POISON"

Flea-killers are poisonous. You should not spray these toxic chemicals on areas of a dog's body that he licks, including his genitals and his face. Flea killers taken internally are a better answer, but check with your vet in case internal therapy is not advised for your dog.

LIFE CYCLE STAGES

During its life, a flea will pass through four life stages: egg, larva, pupa or nymph and adult. The adult stage is the most visible and irritating stage of the flea life cycle, and this is why the majority of flea-control products concentrate on this stage. The fact is that adult fleas account for only 1% of the total flea population, and the other 99% exist in pre-adult stages, i.e., eggs, larvae and nymphs. The pre-adult stages are barely visible to the naked eye.

THE LIFE CYCLE OF THE FLEA

Eggs are laid on the dog, usually in quantities of about 20 or 30, several times a day. The adult female flea must have a blood meal before each egg-laying session. When first laid, the eggs will cling to the dog's hair, as the eggs are still moist. However, they will quickly dry out and fall from the dog, especially if the dog moves around or scratches. Many eggs will fall off in the dog's favorite area or an area in which he spends a lot of time, such as his bed.

Once the eggs fall from the dog onto the carpet or furniture, they will hatch into larvae. This takes from one to ten days. Larvae are not particularly mobile and will usually travel only a few inches from where they hatch. However, they do have a tendency to move away from bright light and heavy

> **EN GARDE:**
> **CATCHING FLEAS OFF GUARD!**
> Consider the following ways to arm yourself against fleas:
> - Add a small amount of pennyroyal or eucalyptus oil to your dog's bath. These natural remedies repel fleas.
> - Supplement your dog's food with fresh garlic (minced or grated) and a hearty amount of brewer's yeast, both of which ward off fleas.
> - Use a flea comb on your dog daily. Submerge fleas in a cup of bleach to kill them quickly.
> - Confine the dog to only a few rooms to limit the spread of fleas in the home.
> - Vacuum daily...and get all of the crevices! Dispose of the bag every few days until the problem is under control.
> - Wash your dog's bedding daily. Cover cushions where your dog sleeps with towels, and wash the towels often.

traffic—under furniture and behind doors are common places to find high quantities of flea larvae.

The flea larvae feed on dead organic matter, including adult flea feces, until they are ready to change into adult fleas. Fleas will usually remain as larvae for around seven days. After this period, the larvae will pupate into protective pupae. While inside the pupae, the larvae will undergo

Fleas have been measured as being able to jump 300,000 times and can jump over 150 times their length in any direction, including straight up.

metamorphosis and change into adult fleas. This can take as little time as a few days, but the adult fleas can remain inside the pupae waiting to hatch for up to two years. The pupae are signaled to hatch by certain stimuli, such as physical pressure—the pupae's being stepped on, heat from an animal's lying on the pupae or increased carbon-dioxide levels and vibrations—indicating that a suitable host is available.

Once hatched, the adult flea must feed within a few days. Once the adult flea finds a host, it will not leave voluntarily. It only becomes dislodged by grooming or the host animal's scratching.

PHOTO BY DWIGHT R. KUHN

The adult flea will remain on the host for the duration of its life unless forcibly removed.

TREATING THE ENVIRONMENT AND THE DOG

Treating fleas should be a two-pronged attack. First, the environment needs to be treated; this includes carpets and furniture, especially the dog's bedding and areas underneath furniture. The environment should be treated with a household spray containing an Insect Growth Regulator (IGR) and an insecticide to kill the adult fleas. Most IGRs are effective against eggs and larvae; they actually mimic the fleas' own hormones and stop the eggs and larvae from developing into adult fleas. There are currently no treatments available to attack the pupa stage of the life cycle, so the adult insecticide is used to kill the newly hatched adult fleas before they find a host. Most IGRs are active for many months, while

A scanning electron micrograph of a dog or cat flea, *Ctenocephalides,* magnified more than 100x. This image has been colorized for effect.

S. E. M. BY DR DENNIS KUNKEL, UNIVERSITY OF HAWAII

THE LIFE CYCLE OF THE FLEA

Adult

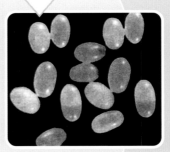

Egg

Larva

**Pupa
or
Nymph**

A LOOK AT FLEAS

Fleas have been around for millions of years and have adapted to changing host animals. They are able to go through a complete life cycle in less than one month or they can extend their lives to almost two years by remaining as pupae or cocoons. They do not need blood or any other food for up to 20 months.

INSECT GROWTH REGULATOR (IGR)

Two types of products should be used when treating fleas—a product to treat the pet and a product to treat the home. Adult fleas represent less than 1% of the flea population. The pre-adult fleas (eggs, larvae and pupae) represent more than 99% of the flea population and are found in the environment; it is in the case of pre-adult fleas that products containing an Insect Growth Regulator (IGR) should be used in the home.

IGRs are a new class of compounds used to prevent the development of insects. They do not kill the insect outright, but instead use the insect's biology against it to stop it from completing its growth. Products that contain methoprene are the world's first and leading IGRs. Used to control fleas and other insects, this type of IGR will stop flea larvae from developing and protect the house for up to seven months.

adult insecticides are only active for a few days.

When treating with a household spray, it is a good idea to vacuum before applying the product. This stimulates as many pupae as possible to hatch into adult fleas. The vacuum cleaner should also be treated with an insecticide to prevent the eggs and larvae that have been collected in the vacuum bag from hatching.

The second stage of treatment is to apply an adult insecticide to the dog. Traditionally, this would be in the form of a collar or a spray, but more recent innovations include digestible insecticides that poison the fleas when they ingest the dog's blood. Alternatively, there are drops that, when placed on the back of the dog's neck, spread throughout the dog's hair and skin to kill adult fleas.

TICKS

Though not as common as fleas, ticks are found all over the tropical and temperate world. They don't bite, like fleas; they harpoon. They dig their sharp proboscis (nose) into the dog's skin and drink the blood. Their

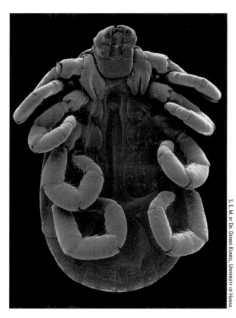

only food and drink is dog's blood. Dogs can get Lyme disease, Rocky Mountain spotted fever, tick bite paralysis and many other diseases from ticks. They may live where fleas are found and they like to hide in cracks or seams in walls. They are controlled the same way fleas are controlled.

The American dog tick, *Dermacentor variabilis*, may well be the most common dog tick in many geographical areas, especially those areas where the climate is hot and humid. Most dog ticks have life expectancies of a week to six months, depending upon climatic conditions. They can neither jump nor fly, but they can crawl slowly and can range up to 16 feet to reach a sleeping or unsuspecting dog.

MITES

Just as fleas and ticks can be problematic for your dog, mites can also lead to an itchy nuisance. Microscopic in size, mites are related to ticks and generally take up permanent residence on their host animal— in this case, your dog! The term *mange* refers to any infestation caused by one of the mighty mites, of which there are six varieties that concern dog owners.

Demodex mites cause a condition known as demodicosis

DEER-TICK CROSSING

The great outdoors may be fun for your dog, but it also is home to dangerous ticks. Deer ticks carry a bacterium known as *Borrelia burgdorferi* and are most active in the autumn and spring. When infections are caught early, penicillin and tetracycline are effective antibiotics, but, if left untreated, the bacteria may cause neurological, kidney and cardiac problems as well as long-term trouble with walking and painful joints.

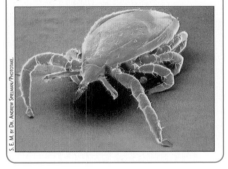

S. E. M. BY DR. ANDREW SPELMAN/PHOTOTAKE.

PHOTO BY DR. DENNIS KUNKEL, UNIVERSITY OF HAWAII.

The head of an American dog tick, *Dermacentor variabilis*, enlarged and colorized for effect.

The mange mite, *Psoroptes bovis*, can infest cattle and other domestic animals.

The mange mite, *Psoroptes bovis*, can infest cattle and other domestic animals.

PHOTO BY JAMES HAYDEN/YOAV/PHOTOTAKE.

Human lice look like dog lice; the two are closely related.

PHOTO BY DWIGHT R. KUHN.

(sometimes called red mange or follicular mange), in which the mites live in the dog's hair follicles and sebaceous glands in larger-than-normal amounts. This type of mange is commonly passed from the dam to her puppies and usually shows up on the puppies' muzzles, though demodicosis is not transferable from one normal dog to another. Most dogs recover from this type of mange without any treatment, though topical therapies are commonly prescribed by the vet.

The *Cheyletiellosis* mite is the hook-mouthed culprit associated with "walking dandruff," a condition that affects dogs as well as cats and rabbits. This mite lives on the surface of the animal's skin and is readily transferable through direct or indirect contact with an affected animal. The dandruff is present in the form of scaly skin, which may or may not be itchy. If not treated, this mange can affect a whole kennel of dogs and can be spread to humans as well.

The *Sarcoptes* mite causes intense itching on the dog in the form of a condition known as scabies or sarcoptic mange. The cycle of the *Sarcoptes* mite lasts about three weeks, and the mites live in the top layer of the dog's skin (epidermis), preferably in areas with little hair. Scabies is highly contagious and can be passed to humans. Sometimes an allergic reaction to the mite worsens the severe itching associated with sarcoptic mange.

Ear mites, *Otodectes cynotis,* lead to otodectic mange, which most commonly affects the outer ear canal of the dog, though other areas can be affected as well. Dogs with ear-mite infestation commonly scratch at their ears, causing further irritation, and shake their heads. Dark brown droppings in the outer ear confirm the diagnosis. Your vet can prescribe a treatment to flush out the ears and kill any eggs in the ears. A complete month of treatment is necessary to cure the mange.

Two other mites, less common in dogs, include *Dermanyssus gallinae* (the poultry or red mite) and *Eutrombicula alfreddugesi* (the North American mite associated with trombiculidiasis or chigger infestation). The poultry mite frequently lives on chickens, but can transfer to dogs who spend time near farm animals. Chigger infestation affects dogs in the

NOT A DROP TO DRINK

Never allow your dog to swim in polluted water or public areas where water quality can be suspect. Even perfectly clear water can harbor parasites, many of which can cause serious to fatal illnesses in canines. Areas inhabited by waterfowl and other wildlife are especially dangerous.

central US who have exposure to woodlands. The types of mange caused by both of these mites are treatable by veterinarians.

INTERNAL PARASITES

Most animals—fishes, birds and mammals, including dogs and humans—have worms and other parasites that live inside their bodies. According to Dr. Herbert R. Axelrod, the fish pathologist, there are two kinds of parasites: dumb and smart. The smart parasites live in peaceful cooperation with their hosts (symbiosis), while the dumb parasites kill their hosts. Most worm infections are relatively easy to control. If they are not controlled, they weaken the host dog to the point that other medical problems occur, but they do not kill the host as dumb parasites would.

DO NOT MIX

Never mix parasite-control products without first consulting your vet. Some products can become toxic when combined with others and can cause fatal consequences.

A brown dog tick, *Rhipicephalus sanguineus*, is an uncommon but annoying tick found on dogs.

Photo by Carolina Biological Supply/Phototake.

Photo by Carolina Biological Supply/Phototake.

The roundworm *Rhabditis* can infect both dogs and humans.

The roundworm, *Ascaris lumbricoides.*

ROUNDWORMS

Average-size dogs can pass 1,360,000 roundworm eggs every day. For example, if there were only 1 million dogs in the world, the world would be saturated with thousands of tons of dog feces. These feces would contain around 15,000,000,000 roundworm eggs.

Up to 31% of home yards and children's sand boxes contain roundworm eggs.

Flushing dog's feces down the toilet is not a safe practice because the usual sewage treatments do not destroy roundworm eggs.

Infected puppies start shedding roundworm eggs at three weeks of age. They can be infected by their mother's milk.

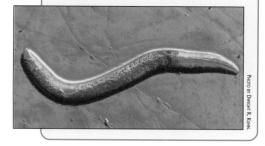

Photo by Dwight R. Kuhn.

ROUNDWORMS

The roundworms that infect dogs are known scientifically as *Toxocara canis.* They live in the dog's intestines and shed eggs continually. It has been estimated that a dog produces about 6 or more ounces of feces every day. Each ounce of feces averages hundreds of thousands of roundworm eggs. There are no known areas in which dogs roam that do not contain roundworm eggs. The greatest danger of roundworms is that they infect people, too! It is wise to have your dog tested regularly for roundworms.

In young puppies, roundworms cause bloated bellies, diarrhea, coughing and vomiting, and are transmitted from the dam (through blood or milk). Affected puppies will not appear as animated as normal puppies. The worms appear spaghetti-like, measuring as long as 6 inches. Adult dogs can acquire roundworms through coprophagia (eating contaminated feces) or by killing rodents that carry roundworms.

Roundworm infection can kill puppies and cause severe problems in adults, as the hatched larvae travel to the lungs and trachea through the bloodstream. Cleanliness is the best preventative for roundworms. Always pick up after your dog and dispose of feces in appropriate receptacles.

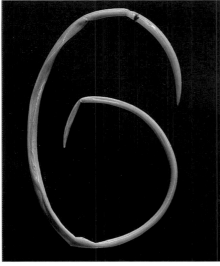

PHOTO BY DWIGHT R. KUHN.

HOOKWORMS

In the United States, dog owners have to be concerned about four different species of hookworm, the most common and most serious of which is *Ancylostoma caninum,* which prefers warm climates. The others are *Ancylostoma braziliense, Ancylostoma tubaeforme* and *Uncinaria stenocephala,* the latter of which is a concern to dogs living in the northern US and Canada, as this species prefers cold climates. Hookworms are dangerous to humans as well as to dogs and cats, and can be the cause of severe anemia due to iron deficiency. The worm uses its teeth to attach itself to the dog's intestines and changes the site of its attachment about six times per day. Each time the worm repositions itself, the dog loses blood and can become anemic. *Ancylostoma caninum* is the most likely of the four species to cause anemia in the dog.

Symptoms of hookworm infection include dark stools, weight loss, general weakness, pale coloration and anemia, as well as possible skin problems. Fortunately, hookworms are easily purged from the affected dog with a number of medications that have proven effective. Discuss these with your veterinarian. Most heartworm preventatives include a hookworm insecticide as well.

Owners also must be aware that hookworms can infect humans, who can acquire the larvae through exposure to contaminated feces. Since the worms cannot complete their life cycle on a human, the worms simply infest the skin and cause irritation. This condition is known as cutaneous larva migrans syndrome. As a preventative, use disposable gloves or a "poop-scoop" to pick up your dog's droppings and prevent your dog (or neighborhood cats) from defecating in children's play areas.

The hookworm, *Ancylostoma caninum.*

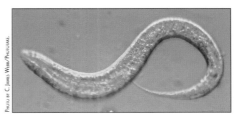

PHOTO BY C. JAMES WEBB/PHOTOTAKE.

The infective stage of the hookworm larva.

TAPEWORMS

Humans, rats, squirrels, foxes, coyotes, wolves and domestic dogs are all susceptible to tapeworm infection. Except in humans, tapeworms are usually not a fatal infection. Infected individuals can harbor 1000 parasitic worms.

Tapeworms, like some other types of worm, are hermaphroditic, meaning male and female in the same worm.

If dogs eat infected rats or mice, or anything else infected with tapeworm, they get the tapeworm disease. One month after attaching to a dog's intestine, the worm starts shedding eggs. These eggs are infective immediately. Infective eggs can live for a few months without a host animal.

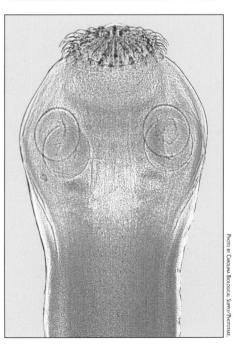

The head and rostellum (the round prominence on the scolex) of a tapeworm, which infects dogs and humans.

PHOTO BY CAROLINA BIOLOGICAL SUPPLY/PHOTOTAKE.

TAPEWORMS

There are many species of tapeworm, all of which are carried by fleas! The most common tapeworm affecting dogs is known as *Dipylidium caninum*. The dog eats the flea and starts the tapeworm cycle. Humans can also be infected with tapeworms—so don't eat fleas! Fleas are so small that your dog could pass them onto your hands, your plate or your food and thus make it possible for you to ingest a flea that is carrying tapeworm eggs.

While tapeworm infection is not life-threatening in dogs (smart parasite!), it can be the cause of a very serious liver disease for humans. About 50% of the humans infected with *Echinococcus multilocularis*, a type of tapeworm that causes alveolar hydatid, perish.

WHIPWORMS

In North America, whipworms are counted among the most common parasitic worms in dogs. The whipworm's scientific name is *Trichuris vulpis*. These worms attach themselves in the lower parts of the intestine, where they feed. Affected dogs may only experience upset tummies, colic and diarrhea. These worms, however, can live for months or years in the dog, beginning their larval stage in the small intestine, spending their adult stage in the large intestine and finally passing infective eggs through the dog's feces. The only way to detect whipworms is through a fecal examination, though this is not always foolproof. Treatment for whipworms is tricky, due to the worms' unusual life-cycle pattern, and very often dogs are reinfected due to exposure to infective eggs on the ground. The whipworm eggs can survive in the environment for as long as five years; thus, cleaning up droppings in your own backyard as well as in public places is absolutely essential for sanitation purposes and the health of your dog and others.

THREADWORMS

Though less common than round-worms, hookworms and those previously mentioned, thread-worms concern dog owners in the southwestern US and Gulf Coast area, where the climate is hot and humid. Living in the small intestine of the dog, this worm measures a mere 2 millimeters and is round in shape. Like that of the whipworm, the threadworm's life cycle is very complex and the eggs and larvae are passed through the feces. A deadly disease in humans, *Strongyloides* readily infects people, and the handling of feces is the most common means of trans-mission. Threadworms are most often seen in young puppies; bloody diarrhea and pneumonia are symptoms. Sick puppies must be isolated and treated immediately; vets recommend a follow-up treat-ment one month later.

HEARTWORM PREVENTATIVES

There are many heartworm preventatives on the market, many of which are sold at your veterinarian's office. These products can be given daily or monthly, depending on the manufacturer's instructions. All of these preventatives contain chemical insecticides directed at killing heartworms, which leads to some controversy among dog owners. In effect, heartworm preventatives are neces-sary evils, though you should determine how necessary based on your pet's lifestyle. There is no doubt that heartworm is a dreadful disease that threatens the lives of dogs. However, the likelihood of your dog's being bitten by an infected mosquito is slim in most places, and a mosquito-repellent (or an herbal remedy such as Wormwood or Black Walnut) is much safer for your dog and will not compromise his immune system (the way heartworm preventatives will). Should you decide to use the tradi-tional preventative "medications," you can consider giving the pill every other or third month. Since the toxins in the pill will kill the heartworms at all stages of develop-ment, the pill would be effective in killing larvae, nymphs or adults and it takes four months for the larvae to reach the adult stage. Thus, there is no rationale to poison-ing the dog's system on a monthly basis. Lastly, do not give the pill during the winter months since there are no mosquitoes around to pass on their infection, unless you live in a tropical environment.

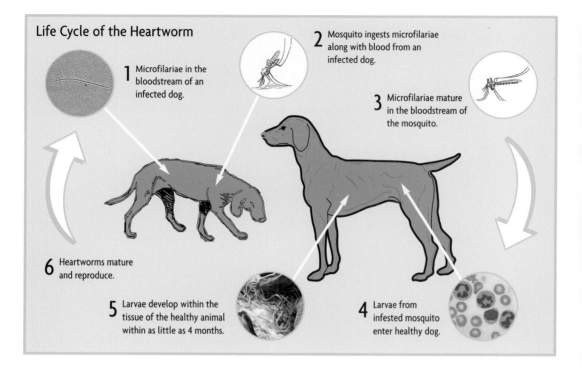

Life Cycle of the Heartworm

1 Microfilariae in the bloodstream of an infected dog.

2 Mosquito ingests microfilariae along with blood from an infected dog.

3 Microfilariae mature in the bloodstream of the mosquito.

4 Larvae from infested mosquito enter healthy dog.

5 Larvae develop within the tissue of the healthy animal within as little as 4 months.

6 Heartworms mature and reproduce.

HEARTWORMS

Heartworms are thin, extended worms up to 12 inches long, which live in a dog's heart and the major blood vessels surrounding it. Dogs may have up to 200 worms. Symptoms may be loss of energy, loss of appetite, coughing, the development of a pot belly and anemia.

Heartworms are transmitted by mosquitoes. The mosquito drinks the blood of an infected dog and takes in larvae with the blood. The larvae, called microfilariae, develop within the body of the mosquito and are passed on to the next dog bitten after the larvae mature. It takes two to three weeks for the larvae to develop to the infective stage within the body of the mosquito. Dogs are usually treated at about six weeks of age and maintained on a prophylactic dose given monthly.

Blood testing for heartworms is not necessarily indicative of how seriously your dog is infected. Although this is a dangerous disease, it is not easy for a dog to be infected. Discuss the various preventatives with your vet, as there are many different types now available. Together you can decide on a safe course of prevention for your dog.

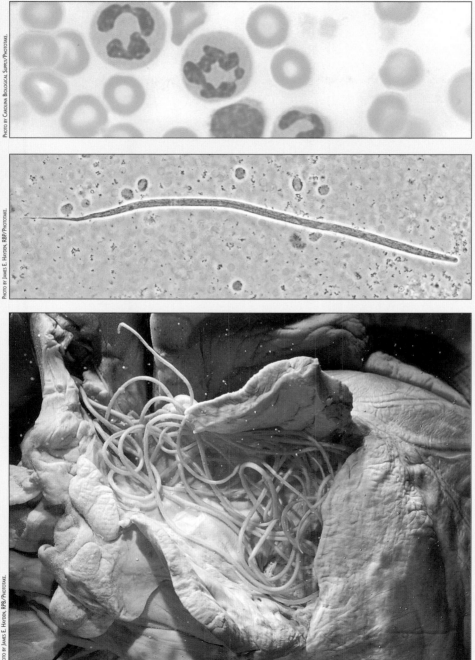

Magnified heart-
worm larvae,
Dirofilaria immitis.

Heartworm,
*Dirofilaria
immitis.*

The heart
of a dog infected
with canine heart-
worm, *Dirofilaria
immitis.*

CDS: COGNITIVE DYSFUNCTION SYNDROME
"Old-Dog Syndrome"

There are many ways for you to evaluate old-dog syndrome. Veterinarians have defined CDS (cognitive dysfunction syndrome) as the gradual deterioration of cognitive abilities. These are indicated by changes in the dog's behavior. When a dog changes his routine response, and maladies have been eliminated as the cause of these behavioral changes, then CDS is the usual diagnosis.

More than half the dogs over eight years old suffer from some form of CDS. The older the dog, the more chance he has of suffering from CDS. In humans, doctors often dismiss the CDS behavioral changes as part of "winding down."

There are four major signs of CDS: frequent potty accidents inside the home, sleeping much more or much less than normal, acting confused and failing to respond to social stimuli.

SYMPTOMS OF CDS

FREQUENT POTTY ACCIDENTS
- *Urinates in the house.*
- *Defecates in the house.*
- *Doesn't signal that he wants to go out.*

SLEEP PATTERNS
- *Awakens more slowly.*
- *Sleeps more than normal during the day.*
- *Sleeps less during the night.*

CONFUSION
- *Goes outside and just stands there.*
- *Appears confused with a faraway look in his eyes.*
- *Hides more often.*
- *Doesn't recognize friends.*
- *Doesn't come when called.*
- *Walks around listlessly and without a destination.*

FAILURE TO RESPOND TO SOCIAL STIMULI
- *Comes to people less frequently, whether called or not.*
- *Doesn't tolerate petting for more than a short time.*
- *Doesn't come to the door when you return home.*

CAVALIER KING CHARLES SPANIEL

The term *old* is a qualitative term. For dogs, as well as their masters, old is relative. Certainly we can all distinguish between a puppy Cavalier King Charles Spaniel and an adult Cavalier King Charles Spaniel—there are the obvious physical traits, such as size, appearance and facial expressions, and personality traits. Puppies and young dogs like to play with children. Children's natural exuberance is a good match for the seemingly endless energy of young dogs. They like to run, jump, chase and retrieve. When dogs grow up and cease their interaction with children, they are often thought of as being too old to play with the kids. On the other hand, if a Cavalier King Charles Spaniel is only exposed to less active

people, his life will normally be less active and it will not seem to be getting old as his activity level slows down.

If people live to be 100 years old, dogs live to be 20 years old. While this may seem like a good rule of thumb, it is very inaccurate. When trying to compare dog years to human years, you cannot

Your senior Cavalier deserves special attention from his owners. As the dog ages, his world slows down. You owe it to your pal to be there for him in every way possible.

GETTING OLD

The bottom line is simply that a dog is getting old when you think he is getting old because he slows down in his general activities, including walking, running, eating, jumping and retrieving. On the other hand, certain activities increase, like more sleeping, more barking and more repetition of habits like going to the door when you put your coat on without being called.

Your veterinarian can evaluate your senior Cavalier and recommend a preventative health-care program suited to your aging dog.

make a generalization about all dogs. You can make the generalization that 14 years is a good lifespan for a Cavalier King Charles Spaniel, which is quite good compared to, say, a Great Dane. Many large breeds typically live for fewer years than smaller ones. Dogs are generally considered mature within three years, but they can reproduce even earlier. So the first three years of a dog's life are like seven times that of comparable humans. That means a 3-year-old dog is like a 21-year-old human. As the curve of comparison shows, there is no hard and fast rule for comparing dog and

human ages. The comparison is made even more difficult, for not all humans age at the same rate...and human females live longer than human males.

WHAT TO LOOK FOR IN SENIORS

Most veterinarians and behaviorists use the seven-year mark as the time to consider a dog a senior. The term *senior* does not imply that the dog is geriatric and has begun to fail in mind and body. Aging is essentially a slowing process. Humans readily admit that they feel a difference in their activity level from age 20

SIGNS OF AGING

An old dog starts to show one or more of the following symptoms:

- Sleep patterns are deeper and longer and the old dog is harder to awaken.

- Food intake diminishes.

- Responses to calls, whistles and other signals are ignored more and more.

- Eye contacts do not evoke tail wagging (assuming they once did).

- The hair on his face and paws starts to turn gray. The color breakdown usually starts around the eyes and mouth.

to 30, and then from 30 to 40, etc. By treating the seven-year-old dog as a senior, owners are able to implement certain therapeutic and preventative medical strategies with the help of their veterinarians. A senior-care program should include at least two veterinary visits per year, screening sessions to determine the dog's health status, as well as nutritional counseling. Veterinarians determine the senior dog's health status through a blood smear for a complete blood count, serum chemistry profile with electrolytes, urinalysis, blood pressure check, electrocardiogram, ocular tonometry (pressure on the eyeball) and dental prophylaxis.

Such an extensive program for senior dogs is well advised before owners start to see the obvious physical signs of aging, such as slower and inhibited move-

Like humans, dogs age at different rates. It is entirely possible for your Cavalier not to show signs of aging until he is ten or more. Nonetheless, be wary of his changing needs and behavior.

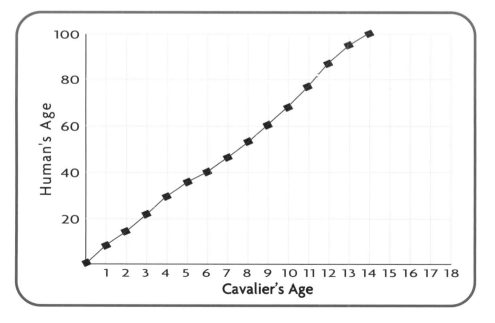

ment, graying, increased sleep/nap periods, and disinterest in play and other activity. This preventative program promises a longer, healthier life for the aging dog. Among the physical problems common in aging dogs are the loss of sight and hearing, arthritis, kidney and liver failure, diabetes mellitus, heart disease and Cushing's disease (a hormonal disease).

In addition to the physical manifestations discussed, there are some behavioral changes and problems related to aging dogs. Dogs suffering from hearing or vision loss, dental discomfort or arthritis can become aggressive. Likewise the near-deaf and/or blind dog may be startled more easily and react in an unexpectedly aggressive manner. Seniors suffering from senility can become more impatient and irritable. Housesoiling accidents are associated with loss of mobility, kidney problems, loss of sphincter control as well as plaque accumulation, physiological brain changes and reactions to medications.

Older dogs, just like young puppies, suffer from separation anxiety, which can lead to excessive barking, whining, housesoiling, and destructive behavior. Seniors may become fearful of everyday sounds, such as vacuum cleaners, heaters, thunder, and passing traffic. Some dogs have difficulty sleeping, due to discomfort, the need for frequent potty visits, and the like.

Owners should avoid spoiling the older dog with too many fatty treats. Obesity is a common problem in older dogs and subtracts years from their lives. Keep the senior dog as trim as possible since excessive weight puts additional stress on the body's vital organs. Some breeders recommend supplementing

NOTICING THE SYMPTOMS

The symptoms listed below are symptoms that gradually appear and become more noticeable. They are not life-threatening; however, the symptoms below are to be taken very seriously and warrant a discussion with your veterinarian:

- Your dog cries and whimpers when he moves, and he stops running completely.
- Convulsions start or become more serious and frequent. The usual convulsion (spasm) is when the dog stiffens and starts to tremble, being unable or unwilling to move. The seizure usually lasts for 5 to 30 minutes.
- Your dog drinks more water and urinates more frequently. Wetting and bowel accidents take place indoors without warning.
- Vomiting becomes more and more frequent.

the diet with foods high in fiber and lower in calories. Adding fresh vegetables and marrow broth to the senior's diet makes a tasty, low-calorie, low-fat supplement. Vets also offer specialty diets for senior dogs that are worth exploring.

Your dog, as he nears his twilight years, needs his owner's patience and good care more than ever. Never punish an older dog for an accident or abnormal behavior. For all of the years of love and companionship that your dog has provided, he deserves special attention and courtesies. The older dog may need to relieve himself at 3 a.m. because he can no longer hold it for eight hours. Older dogs may not be able to remain crated for more than two or three hours. It may be time to give up a sofa or chair to your old friend. Although he may not seem as enthusiastic about your attention and petting, he does appreciate the considerations you offer as he gets older.

Your Cavalier King Charles Spaniel does not understand why his world is slowing down. Owners must make the transition into the golden years as pleasant and rewarding as possible.

WHAT TO DO WHEN THE TIME COMES

You are never fully prepared to make a rational decision about

> ### SMELLING YOUR AGE
>
> Your senior dog may lose interest in eating, not because he's less hungry but because his senses of smell and taste have diminished. The old chow simply does not smell as good as it once did. Additionally, older dogs use less energy and thereby can sustain themselves on less food.

putting your dog to sleep. It is very obvious that you love your Cavalier King Charles Spaniel or you would not be reading this book. Putting a loved dog to sleep is extremely difficult. It is a decision that must be made with your veterinarian. You are usually forced to make the decision when one of the life-threatening symptoms listed above becomes serious enough for you to seek veterinary help. If the prognosis of the malady indicates the end is near and your beloved pet will only suffer more and experience no enjoyment for the balance of his life, then euthanasia is the right choice.

WHAT IS EUTHANASIA?

Euthanasia derives from the Greek, meaning *good death*. In other words, it means the planned, painless killing of a dog suffering from a painful, incurable condition, or who is so aged that he cannot walk, see, eat or control his excretory functions.

There are pet cemeteries to be found in most areas of the world.

Photo by Bill Jonas.

Euthanasia is usually accomplished by injection with an overdose of an anesthesia or barbiturate. Aside from the prick of the needle, the experience is usually painless.

MAKING FINAL DECISIONS

The decision to euthanize your dog is never easy. The days during which the dog becomes ill and the end occurs can be unusu-ally stressful for you. If this is your first experience with the death of a loved one, you may need the comfort dictated by your religious beliefs. If you are the head of the family and have children, you should have involved them in the decision of putting your Cavalier King Charles Spaniel to sleep. Usually your dog can be maintained on drugs for a few days in order to give you ample time to make a decision. During this time, talking with members of your family or even people who have lived through this same experience can ease the burden of your inevitable decision.

THE FINAL RESTING PLACE

Dogs can have some of the same privileges as humans. They can occasionally be buried in their entirety in a pet cemetery which is generally expensive, or if they have died at home can be buried in your yard in a place suitably marked with some stone or newly planted tree or bush. Alternatively they can be cremated and the ashes returned to you, or some people prefer to leave their dogs at the vet's office for the vet to dispose of.

All of these options should be discussed frankly and openly with your veterinarian. Do not be afraid to ask financial questions. Individual cremations are costly, but a less expensive option is mass cremation, although of course the ashes can not then be returned. Vets can usually arrange cremation services on your behalf.

GETTING ANOTHER DOG?

The grief of losing your beloved dog will be as lasting as the grief of losing a human friend or relative. In most cases, if your dog died of old age (if there is such a thing), he had slowed down considerably. Do you want a new Cavalier King Charles Spaniel puppy to replace him? Or are you better off in finding a more mature Cavalier King Charles Spaniel, say two to three years of age, which will usually be house-trained and will have an already developed personality. In this case, you can find out if you like each other after a few hours of being together.

The decision is, of course, your own. Do you want another Cavalier King Charles Spaniel or perhaps a different breed so as to avoid comparison with your beloved friend? Most people usually choose the same breed because they know and love the characteristics of that breed. Then, too, they often know people who have the same breed and perhaps they are lucky enough that one of their friends expects a litter soon. What could be better?

There are places in some pet cemeteries where your dog's ashes can be kept.

CAVALIER KING CHARLES SPANIEL

When you purchase your Cavalier, you will make it clear to the breeder whether you want one just as a lovable companion and pet, or if you hope to be buying a Cavalier with show prospects. No reputable breeder will sell you a young puppy and tell you that it is *definitely* of show quality, for so much can go wrong during the early months of a puppy's development. If you plan to show, what you will hopefully have acquired is a puppy with "show potential."

To the novice, exhibiting a Cavalier in the show ring may look easy, but it takes a lot of hard work and devotion to do top winning at a show such as the prestigious Westminster Kennel Club dog show, not to mention a little luck, too!

The first concept that the canine novice learns when watch-

Medals are issued at many prestigious dog competitions.

ing a dog show is that each dog first competes against members of his own breed. Once the judge has selected the best member of each breed (Best of Breed), provided that the show is judged on a Group system, that chosen dog will compete with other dogs in his group. Finally, the dogs chosen first in each group will compete for Best in Show.

The second concept that you must understand is that the dogs are not actually compared against one another. The judge compares each dog against his breed standard, the

AKC GROUPS

For showing purposes, the American Kennel Club divides its recognized breeds into seven groups: Sporting Dogs, Hounds, Working Dogs, Terriers, Toys, Non-Sporting Dogs and Herding Dogs.

written description of the ideal specimen that is approved by the American Kennel Club (AKC). While some early breed standards were indeed based on specific dogs that were famous or popular, many dedicated enthusiasts say that a perfect specimen, as described in the standard, has never walked into a show ring, has never been bred and, to the woe of dog breeders around the globe, does not exist. Breeders attempt to get as close to this ideal as possible with every litter, but theoretically the "perfect" dog is so elusive that it is impossible.

If you are interested in exploring the world of dog showing, your best bet is to join your local breed club or the national parent club, which is the American Cavalier King Charles Spaniel

Club. The Cavalier King Charles Spaniel Club, USA, which is the older of the two clubs, is not the breed's parent club, but functions as a registry. Both these national clubs host regional and national specialties, shows only for Cavaliers, which can include conformation as well as obedience and agility trials. Even if you have no intention of competing with your Cavalier, a specialty is like a festival for lovers of the breed who congregate to share their favorite topic: Cavaliers! Clubs also send out newsletters, and some organize training days and seminars in order that people may learn more about their chosen breed. To locate the breed club closest to you, contact the American Kennel Club (AKC),

The Cavalier King Charles Spaniel makes a fabulous show dog. If you have acquired a puppy with the intentions of showing, you will need to become acquainted with the procedures of the American Kennel Club.

BECOMING A CHAMPION

An official AKC champion of record requires that a dog accumulate 15 points under three different judges, including two "majors" under different judges. Points are awarded based on the number of dogs entered into competition, varying from breed to breed and place to place. A win of three, four or five points is considered a "major." The AKC annually assigns a schedule of points to adjust the variations that accompany a breed's popularity and the population of a given area.

Dog show folk are quite innovative at protecting their Cavalier's coats from the elements. Often vendors sell unique products at the show site, like this doggie coat.

four- or five-point win, and the number of points per win is determined by the number of dogs entered in the show on that day. Depending on the breed, the number of points that are awarded varies. More dogs are needed to rack up the points in more popular breeds, and fewer dogs are needed in less popular breeds.

At any dog show, only one dog and one bitch of each breed can win points. Dog showing does not offer "co-ed" classes. Dogs and bitches never compete against each other in the classes. Non-

which furnishes the rules and regulations for all of these events plus general dog registration and other basic requirements of dog ownership.

The AKC offers three kinds of conformation shows: an all-breed show (for all AKC-recognized breeds), a specialty show (for one breed only, usually sponsored by the parent club) and a Group show (for all breeds in the group). The Cavalier competes in the Toy Group, and there are fabulous Toys-only specialties for the Cavalier to attend and compete in.

For a dog to become an AKC champion of record, the dog must accumulate 15 points at the shows from at least three different judges, including two "majors." A "major" is defined as a three-,

SHOW-RING ETIQUETTE

Just as with anything else, there is a certain etiquette to the show ring that can only be learned through experience. Showing your dog can be quite intimidating to you as a novice when it seems as if everyone else knows what he is doing. You can familiarize yourself with ring procedure beforehand by taking showing classes to prepare you and your dog for conformation showing and by talking with experienced handlers. When you are in the ring, it is very important to pay attention and listen to the instructions you are given by the judge about where to move your dog. Remember, even the most skilled handlers had to start somewhere. Keep it up and you too will become a proficient handler as you gain practice and experience.

champion dogs are called "class dogs" because they compete in one of five classes. Dogs are entered in a particular class depending on age and previous show wins. To begin, there is the Puppy Class (for 6- to 9-month-olds and for 9- to 12-month-olds); this class is followed by the Novice Class (for dogs that have not won any first prizes except in the Puppy Class or three first prizes in the Novice Class and have not accumulated any points toward their champion title); the Bred-by-Exhibitor Class (for dogs handled by their breeders or by one of the breeder's immediate family); the American-bred Class (for dogs bred in the US); and the Open Class (for any dog that is not a champion).

The judge at the show begins judging the Puppy Class, first dogs and then bitches, and proceeds through the classes. The judge places his winners first through fourth in each class. In the Winners Class, the first-place winners of each class compete with one another to determine Winners Dog and Winners Bitch. The judge also places a Reserve Winners Dog and Reserve Winners Bitch, which could be awarded the points in the case of a disqual-ification. The Winners Dog and Winners Bitch—the two that are awarded the points for the breed—then compete with any champions of record (often called "specials")

> **FIVE CLASSES AT SHOWS**
>
> At most AKC all-breed shows, there are five regular classes offered: Puppy, Novice, Bred-by-Exhibitor, American-bred and Open. The Puppy Class is usually divided as 6 to 9-months of age and 9 to 12-months of age. When deciding in which class to enter your dog, male or female, you must care-fully check the show schedule to make sure that you have selected the right class. Depending on the age of the dog, its previ-ous first-place wins and the sex of the dog, you must make the best choice. It is possible to enter a one-year-old dog who has not won suffi-cient first places in any of the non-Puppy Classes, though the competition is more intense the further you progress from the Puppy Class.

entered in the show. The judge reviews the Winners Dog, Winners Bitch and all of the champions to select his Best of Breed. The Best of Winners is selected between the Winners Dog and Winners Bitch. Were one of these two to be selected Best of Breed, it would automatically be named Best of Winners as well. Finally the judge selects his Best of Opposite Sex to the Best of Breed winner.

At a Group show or all-breed show, the Best of Breed winners from each breed then compete

There are many kinds of dog shows and competitions in which you can enter your Cavalier. Your breeder should be able to help introduce you to the joys of dog showing.

against one another for Group One through Group Four. The judge compares each Best of Breed to his breed standard, and the dog that most closely lives up to the ideal for his breed is selected as Group One. Finally, all seven group winners (from the Toy Group, Working Group, Hound Group, etc.) compete for Best in Show.

To find out about dog shows in your area, you can subscribe to the American Kennel Club's monthly magazine, the *American Kennel Gazette* and the accompanying *Events Calendar*. You can also look in your local newspaper for advertisements for dog shows in your area or go on the Internet to the AKC's website, http:www.akc.org.

If your Cavalier is six months of age or older and registered with the AKC, you can enter him in a dog show where the breed is offered classes. Provided that your Cavalier does not have a disqualifying fault, he can compete. Only unaltered dogs can be entered in a dog show, so if you have spayed or neutered your Cavalier, your dog

CANINE GOOD CITIZEN® PROGRAM

Have you ever considered getting your dog "certified"? The AKC's Canine Good Citizen® Program affords your dog just that opportunity. Your dog shows that he is a well-behaved canine citizen, using the basic training and good manners you have taught him, by taking a series of ten tests that illustrate that he can behave properly at home, in a public place and around other dogs. The tests are administered by participating dog clubs, colleges, 4-H clubs, scouts and other community groups and are open to all pure-bred and mixed-breed dogs. Upon passing the ten tests, the suffix CGC is then applied to your dog's name.

The ten tests are: 1. Accepting a friendly stranger; 2. Sitting politely for petting; 3. Appearance and grooming; 4. Walking on a lead; 5. Walking through a group of people; 6. Sit, down and stay on command; 7. Coming when called; 8. Meeting another dog; 9. Calm reaction to distractions; 10. Separation from owner.

cannot compete in conformation shows. The reason for this is simple. Dog shows are the main forum to prove which representatives in a breed are worthy of being bred. Only dogs that have achieved championships—the AKC "seal of approval" for excellence in pure-bred dogs—should be bred. Altered dogs, however, can participate in other AKC events such as obedience trials and the Canine Good Citizen program.

Before you actually step into the ring, you would be well advised to sit back and observe the judge's ring procedure. The judge asks each handler to "stack" the dog, hopefully showing the dog off to his best advantage. The judge will observe the dog from a distance and from different angles, and approach the dog to check his teeth, overall structure, alertness and muscle tone, as well as consider how well the dog

The dogs winning at a conformation show represent many years of competent breeding and training. You should not expect to go home with the ribbons at your first show.

"conforms" to the standard. Most importantly, the judge will have the exhibitor move the dog around the ring in some pattern that he should specify in order to evaluate the dog's gait. Finally, the judge will give the dog one last look before moving on to the next exhibitor.

If you are not in the top four in your class at your first show, do not be discouraged. Be patient and consistent, and you may eventually find yourself in a winning line-up. Remember that the winners were once in your shoes and have devoted many hours and much money to earn the placement. If you find that your dog is losing every time and never getting a nod, it may be time to consider a different dog sport or to just enjoy your Cavalier as a pet. Parent clubs offer other events, such as agility, obedience, instinct tests and more, which may be of interest to the owner of a well-trained Cavalier.

OBEDIENCE TRIALS

Obedience trials in the US trace back to the early 1930s when organized obedience training was developed to demonstrate how well dog and owner could work together. The pioneer of obedience trials is Mrs. Helen Whitehouse Walker, a Standard Poodle fancier, who designed a series of exercises after the Associated Sheep, Police Army Dog Society of Great Britain. Since the days of Mrs.

Walker, obedience trials have grown by leaps and bounds, and today there are over 2,000 trials held in the US every year, with more than 100,000 dogs competing. Any AKC-registered dog can enter an obedience trial, regardless of conformational disqualifications or neutering.

Obedience trials are divided into three levels of progressive difficulty. At the first level, the Novice, dogs compete for the title Companion Dog (CD); at the intermediate level, the Open, dogs compete for the title Companion Dog Excellent (CDX); and at the advanced level, the Utility, dogs compete for the title Utility Dog (UD). Classes are sub-divided into

INFORMATION ON CLUBS
You can get information about dog shows from the national kennel clubs:

American Kennel Club
5580 Centerview Dr., Raleigh, NC 27606-3390
www.akc.org

United Kennel Club
100 E. Kilgore Road, Kalamazoo, MI 49002
www.ukcdogs.com

Canadian Kennel Club
89 Skyway Ave., Suite 100, Etobicoke, Ontario M9W 6R4 Canada
www.ckc.ca

The Kennel Club
1-5 Clarges St., Piccadilly, London W1Y 8AB, UK
www.the-kennel-club.org.uk

"A" (for beginners) and "B" (for more experienced handlers). A perfect score at any level is 200, and a dog must score 170 or better to earn a "leg," of which three are needed to earn the title. To earn points, the dog must score more than 50% of the available points in each exercise; the possible points range from 20 to 40.

Each level consists of a different set of exercises. In the Novice level, the dog must heel on- and off-lead, come, long sit, long down and stand for examination. These skills are the basic ones required for a well-behaved "Companion Dog." The Open level requires that the dog perform the same exercises as in the Novice, but without a leash for extended lengths of time, as well as retrieve a dumbbell, broad jump and drop on recall. In the Utility level, dogs must perform ten difficult exercises, including scent discrimination, hand signals for basic commands, directed jump and directed retrieve.

Once a dog has earned the UD title, he can compete with other proven obedience dogs for the coveted title of Utility Dog Excellent (UDX), which requires that the dog win "legs" in ten shows. Utility Dogs who earn "legs" in Open B and Utility B earn points toward their Obedience Trial Champion title. In 1977, the title Obedience Trial Champion (OTCh.) was established by the AKC. To become an OTCh., a dog needs to earn 100 points, which requires three first places in Open B and Utility under three different judges.

The Grand Prix of obedience trials, the AKC National Obedience Invitational gives qualifying Utility Dogs the chance to win the newest and highest title: National Obedience Champion (NOC). Only the top 25 ranked obedience dogs, plus any dog ranked in the top 3 in his breed, are allowed to compete.

The Cavalier breed is exceptional in many ways. At agility trials, the breed has proven both trainable and athletic. The Cavalier is one of the few Toy breeds that consistently excels in agility trials.

AGILITY TRIALS

Having had its origins in the UK back in 1977, agility had its official AKC beginning in August 1994, when the first licensed agility trials were held. The AKC allows all registered breeds (including Miscellaneous Class breeds) to participate, providing the dog is 12 months of age or older. Agility is designed so that the handler demonstrates how well the dog can work at his side. The handler directs his dog over an obstacle course that includes jumps as well as tires, the dog walk, weave poles, pipe tunnels, collapsed tunnels, etc. While working his way through the course, the dog must keep one eye and ear on the handler and the rest of his body on the course. The handler gives verbal and hand signals to guide the dog through the course.

The first organization to promote agility trials in the US was the United States Dog Agility Association, Inc. (USDAA), which was established in 1986 and spawned numerous member clubs around the country. Both the USDAA and the AKC offer titles to winning dogs. Three titles are available through the USDAA: Agility Dog (AD), Advanced Agility Dog (AAD) and Master Agility Dog (MAD). The AKC offers Novice Agility (NA), Open Agility (OA), Agility Excellent (AX) and Master Agility Excellent (MX). Beyond these four AKC titles, dogs can win additional ones in Jumper agility titles "jumper" classes, Jumpers with Weave Novice (NAJ), Open (OAJ) and Excellent (MXJ), which lead to the ultimate title(s): MACH, Master Agility Champion. Dogs can continue to add number designations to the MACH titles, indicating how many times the dog has met the MACH requirements, such as MACH1, MACH2 and so on.

Agility is great fun for dog and owner with many rewards for everyone involved. Interested owners should join a training club that has obstacles and experienced agility handlers who can introduce you and your dog to the "ropes" (and tires, tunnels, etc.).

Cavaliers can be taught many tricks, especially if there's a tasty treat involved. The time you spend in training your Cavalier will be repaid many times over the lifespan of the dog.

CAVALIER KING CHARLES SPANIEL

As a Cavalier owner, you have selected your dog so that you and your loved ones can have a companion, a footwarmer, a friend and a four-legged family member. You invest time, money and effort to care for and train the family's new charge. Of course, this chosen canine behaves perfectly! Well, perfectly like a dog. When discussing the Cavalier, owners have much to consider. Most behaviorists and trainers regard the Cavalier as a very responsive and smart canine, able to assimilate hundreds of words and dozens of commands. Although not primarily a working or performance dog, the Cavalier is known to excel in both obedience and agility and can be trained to execute many useful tasks.

THINK LIKE A DOG

Dogs do not think like humans, nor do humans think like dogs, though we try. Unfortunately, a dog is incapable of figuring out

Cavaliers do best if they have a lot of love and human companionship. If there are children in your household, encourage them to assist in training your Cavalier.

SMILE!

Dogs and humans may be the only animals that smile. A dog will imitate the smile on his owner's face when he greets a friend. The dog only smiles at his human friends; he never smiles at another dog or cat. Usually, a dog rolls up his lips and shows his teeth in a clenched mouth while rolling over onto his back, begging for a soft scratch.

how humans think, so the responsibility falls on the owner to adopt a proper canine mindset. Dogs cannot rationalize and only exist in the present moment. Many dog owners make the mistake in training of thinking that they can reprimand their dog for something he did a while ago. Basically, you cannot even reprimand a dog for something he did 20 seconds ago! Either catch him in the act or forget it! It is a waste of your and your dog's time—in his mind, you are reprimanding him for whatever he is doing at that moment.

The following behavioral problems represent some which owners most commonly encounter. Every dog is unique and every situation is unique. No author could purport for you to solve your Cavalier's problem simply by reading a chapter in a book. Here we outline some basic "dogspeak" so that owners' chances of solving behavioral problems are increased. Discuss bad habits with your veterinarian

AIN'T MISBEHAVIN'
Punishment is rarely necessary for a misbehaving dog. Dogs that habitually behave badly probably had a poor education and do not know what is expected of them. They need training. Negative reinforcement on your part usually does more harm than good.

and he can recommend a behavioral specialist to consult in appropriate cases. Since behavioral abnormalties are the leading reason owners abandon their pets, we hope that you will make a valiant effort to solve your Cavalier's problem. Patience and understanding are virtues that dwell in every pet-loving household.

AGGRESSION
Aggression can be a very big problem in small dogs, though not so in the Cavalier—thankfully. Aggression, when not controlled, always becomes dangerous. An aggressive dog, no matter the size, may lunge at, bite or even attack a person or another dog. Aggressive behavior is not to be tolerated. It is painful for a family to watch their dog become unpredictable in his behavior to the point where they are afraid of him. While not all aggressive behavior is dangerous, growling, baring teeth, etc., can be frightening: It is important to ascertain why the dog is acting in this manner. Aggression is a display of dominance, and the dog should not have the dominant role in his pack, which is, in this case, your family.

It is important not to challenge an aggressive dog as this could provoke an attack. Observe your Cavalier's body language. Does he make direct eye contact and stare? Does he try to make

about it. An aggressive dog cannot be trusted, and a dog that cannot be trusted is not safe to have as a family pet. If, very unusually, you find that your pet has become untrustworthy and you feel it necessary to seek a new home with a more suitable family and environment, explain fully to the new owners all of your reasons for

himself as large as possible: ears alert, chest out, tail erect? Height and size signify authority in a dog pack—being taller or "above" another dog literally means that he is "above" in the social status. These body signals tell you that your Cavalier thinks he is in charge, a problem that needs to be addressed. An aggressive dog is unpredictable: you never know when he is going to strike out and what he is going to do next. You cannot understand why a dog that is playful and loving one minute is growling and snapping the next.

The best solution is to consult a behavioral specialist, one who has experience with small dogs. Together, perhaps you can pinpoint the cause of your dog's aggression and do something

Fortunately, the Cavalier breed on a whole is among the most amicable of all dogs. Aggression problems have little documentation in the breed.

SOUND BITES

When a dog bites, there is always a good reason for his doing so. Many dogs are trained to protect a person, an area or an object. When that person, area or object is violated, the dog will attack. A dog attacks with his mouth. He has no other means of attack.

Fighting dogs (and there are many breeds which fight) are taught to fight, but they also have a natural instinct to fight. This instinct is normally reserved for other dogs, though unfortunate accidents can occur; for example, when a baby crawls toward a fighting dog and the dog mistakes the crawling child as a potential attacker.

If a dog is a biter for seemingly no reason, if he bites the hand that feeds him or if he snaps at members of your family, see your veterinarian or behaviorist immediately to learn how to modify the dog's behavior.

rehoming the dog to be fair to all concerned. In the very worst case, you will have to consider euthanasia.

AGGRESSION TOWARD OTHER DOGS

A dog's aggressive behavior toward another dog sometimes stems from insufficient exposure to other dogs at an early age. If other dogs make your Cavalier nervous and agitated, he will lash out as a defensive mechanism, though this behavior is thankfully uncommon in the breed. A dog that has not received sufficient exposure to other canines tends to believe that he is the only dog on the planet. The animal becomes so dominant that he does not even show signs that he is fearful or threatened. Without growling or any other physical signal as a warning, he will lunge at and bite

NO EYE CONTACT

DANGER! If you and your on-lead dog are approached by a larger, running dog that is not restrained, walk away from the dog as quickly as possible. Do not allow your dog to make eye contact with the other dog. You should not make eye contact either. In dog terms, eye contact indicates a challenge.

the other dog. A way to correct this is to let your Cavalier approach another dog when walking on lead. Watch very closely and at the very first sign of aggression, correct your Cavalier and pull him away. Scold him for any sign of discomfort, and then praise him when he ignores or tolerates the other dog. Keep this up until he stops the aggressive behavior, learns to ignore the other dog or accepts other dogs. Praise him lavishly for his correct behavior.

DOMINANT AGGRESSION

A social hierarchy is firmly established in a wild dog pack. The dog wants to dominate those under him and please those above him. Dogs know that there must be a leader. If you are not the obvious choice for emperor, the dog will assume the throne! These conflicting innate desires are what a dog owner is up against when he sets about training a dog. In training a dog to obey commands, the owner is reinforcing that he is the top dog in the pack and that the dog should, and should want to, serve his superior. Thus, the owner is suppressing the dog's urge to dominate by modifying his behavior and making him obedient.

An important part of training is taking every opportunity to reinforce that you are the leader. The simple action of making your Cavalier sit to wait for his food

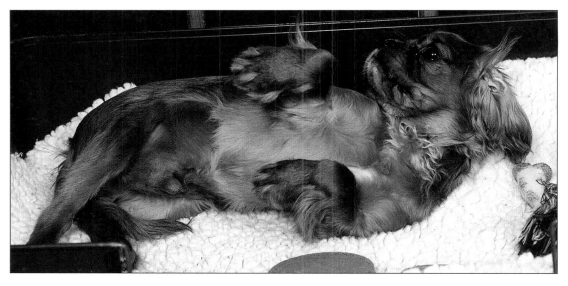

says that you control when he eats and that he is dependent on you for food. Although it may be difficult, do not give in to your dog's wishes every time he whines at you or looks at you with his pleading eyes. It is a constant effort to show the dog that his place in the pack is at the bottom. This is not meant to sound cruel or inhumane. You love your Cavalier and you should treat him with care and affection. You likely did not get a dog just so you could boss around another creature. Dog training is not about being cruel or feeling important, it is about molding the dog's behavior into what is acceptable and teaching him to live by your rules.

In theory, it is quite simple: catch him in appropriate behavior and reward him for it. Add a dog into the equation and it becomes a bit more trying, but as a rule of thumb, positive reinforcement is what works best.

With a dominant dog, punishment and negative reinforcement can have the opposite effect of what you are after. It can make a dog fearful and/or act out aggressively if he feels he is being challenged. Remember, a dominant dog perceives himself at the top of the social heap and will fight to defend his perceived status. The

The ultimate sign of surrender is rolling onto his back and exposing his soft belly. This also shows his human friend trust and submission.

> **TUG-OF-WAR**
> You should never play tug-of-war games with your puppy. Such games create a struggle for top-dog position and teach the puppy that it is okay to challenge you. It will also encourage your puppy's natural tendency to bite down hard and *win*.

best way to prevent that is never to give him reason to think that he is in control in the first place. If you are having trouble training your Cavalier and it seems as if he is constantly challenging your authority, seek the help of an obedience trainer or behavioral specialist. A professional will work with both you and your dog to teach you effective techniques to use at home. Beware of trainers who rely on excessively harsh methods; scolding is necessary now and then, but the focus in your training a dog as sensitive as the Cavalier should always be on positive reinforcement.

If you can isolate what brings out the fear reaction, you can help the dog get over it. Supervise your Cavalier's interactions with people and other dogs, and praise the dog when it goes well. If he starts to act aggressively in a situation, correct him and remove him from the situation. Do not let people approach the dog and start petting him without your express permission. That way, you can have the dog sit to accept petting, and praise him when he behaves properly. You are focusing on praise and on modifying his behavior by rewarding him when he acts appropriately. By being gentle and by supervising his interactions, you are showing him that there is no need to be afraid or defensive.

SEXUAL BEHAVIOR

Dogs exhibit certain sexual behaviors that may have influenced your choice of male or female when you first purchased your Cavalier. To a certain extent, spaying and neutering will eliminate these behaviors, but if you are purchasing a dog that you wish to breed, you should be aware of what you will have to deal with throughout the dog's life.

Female dogs usually have two estruses per year with each season lasting about three weeks. These are the only times in which a female dog will mate, and she usually will not allow this until the second week of the cycle, but this does vary from bitch to bitch. If not bred during the heat cycle, it is not uncommon for a bitch to experience a false pregnancy, in which her mammary glands swell and she exhibits maternal tendencies toward toys or other objects.

Owners must further recognize that mounting is not merely a

DOGGIE DEMOCRACY
Your dog inherited the pack-leader mentality. He only knows about pecking order. He instinctively wants to be top dog, but you have to convince him that you are boss. There is no such thing as living in a democracy with your dog. You are the one who makes the rules.

sexual expression but also one of dominance. Be consistent and persistent and you will find that you can "move mounters."

CHEWING

The national canine pastime is chewing! Every dog loves to sink his "canines" into a tasty bone, but sometimes that bone is in his owner's hand! Dogs need to chew, to massage their gums, to make their new teeth feel better and to exercise their jaws. This is a natural behavior deeply imbedded in all things canine. Your role as owner is not to stop the dog's chewing, but to redirect it to chew-worthy objects. Be an informed owner and purchase top-quality chew toys like strong plastic bones that will not splinter. Be sure that the devices are safe and durable, since your dog's safety is at risk.

Again, the owner is responsible for ensuring a dog-proof environment. The best answer is prevention: that is, put your shoes, handbags and other tasty objects in their proper places (out of the reach of the growing canine mouth) Direct puppies to their toys whenever you see them tasting the furniture legs or the leg of your pants. Make a loud noise to attract the pup's attention and immediately escort him to his chew toy and engage him with the toy for at least four minutes, praising and encouraging him all of the while.

Some trainers recommend deterrents, such as hot pepper or another bitter spice or a product designed for this purpose, to discourage the dog from chewing unwanted objects. Test out these products on your Cav before investing in a large quantity.

JUMPING UP

Jumping up is a dog's friendly way of saying hello! Some dog owners do not mind when their dog jumps up, which is fine for them. The problem arises when guests come to the house and the dog greets them in the same manner—whether they like it or not! However friendly the greeting may be, the chances are that your visitors will not appreciate your dog's enthusiasm. The dog will not be able to distinguish upon whom he can jump and whom he cannot. Therefore, it is probably best to discourage this behavior entirely.

Pick a command such as "Off" (avoid using "Down" since you will use that for the dog to lie down) and tell him "Off" when he jumps up. Place him on the ground on all fours and have him sit, praising him the whole time. Always lavish him with praise and petting when he is in the sit position. That way you are still giving him a warm affectionate greeting, because you are as excited to see him as he is to see you!

A Cavalier should know not to jump up on children, though sometimes, in the excitement of saying hello, even a well-trained dog forgets his education.

DIGGING

Digging, which is seen as a destructive behavior to humans, is actually quite a natural behavior in dogs. Whether or not your dog is one of the "earth dogs" (also known as terriers), his desire to dig can be irrepressible and most frustrating to his owners. When digging occurs in your garden, it

is actually a normal behavior redirected into something the dog can do in his everyday life. In the wild, a dog would be actively seeking food, making his own shelter, etc. He would be using his paws in a purposeful manner for his survival. Since you provide him with food and shelter, he has no need to use his paws for these purposes, and so the energy that he would be using may manifest itself in the form of little holes all over your yard and flower beds.

Perhaps your dog is digging as a reaction to boredom—it is some-

NO JUMPING

Stop a dog from jumping up before he jumps. If he is getting ready to jump onto you, simply walk away. If he jumps up on you before you can turn away, lift your knee so that it bumps him in the chest. Do not be forceful. Your dog soon will realize that jumping up is not a productive way of getting attention.

what similar to someone eating a whole bag of Oreos® in front of the TV—because they are there and there is not anything better to do! Basically, the answer is to provide the dog with adequate play and exercise so that his mind and paws are occupied, and so that he feels as if he is doing something useful.

Of course, digging is easiest to control if it is stopped as soon as possible, but it is often hard to catch a dog in the act. If your dog is a compulsive digger and is not easily distracted by other activities, you can designate an area on your property where it is okay for him to dig. If you catch him digging in an off-limits area of the yard, immediately bring him to the approved area and praise him for digging there. Keep a close eye on him so that you can catch him in the act—that is the only way to make him understand what is permitted and what is not. If you take him to a hole he dug an hour ago and tell him "No," he will understand that you are not fond of holes, dirt or flowers. If you catch him while he is stifle-deep in your tulips, that is when he will get your message.

BARKING

Dogs cannot talk—oh, what they would say if they could! Instead, barking is a dog's way of "talking." It can be somewhat frustrating because it is not always easy

NO KISSES
We all love our dogs and our dogs love us They show their love and affection by licking us. This is not a very sanitary practice, as dogs lick and sniff in some unsavory places. Kissing your dog on the mouth is strictly forbidden, as parasites can be transmitted in this manner.

to tell what a dog means by his bark—is he excited, happy, frightened or angry? Whatever it is that the dog is trying to say, he should not be punished for barking. It is only when the barking becomes excessive, and when the excessive barking becomes a bad habit, that the behavior needs to be modified. Fortunately, Cavaliers tend to use their barks more purposefully than most dogs. If an intruder came into your home in the middle of the night and your Cavalier barked a warning, would not you be pleased? You would probably deem your dog a hero, a wonderful guardian and protector of the home. Most dogs are not as discriminate as the Cavalier. For instance, if a friend drops by unexpectedly and rings the doorbell and is greeted with a sudden sharp bark, you would probably be annoyed at the dog. But in reality, isn't this just the same behavior? The dog does not know any better…unless he sees who is at the door and it is someone he knows, he will bark as a means of vocalizing that his (and your) territory is being threatened. While your friend is not posing a threat, it is all the same to the dog. Barking is his means of letting you know that there is an intrusion, whether friend or foe, on your property. This type of barking is instinctive and should not be discouraged.

Excessive habitual barking, however, is a problem that should be corrected early on. As your Cavalier grows up, you will be able to tell when his barking is purposeful and when it is for no reason. You will become able to distinguish your dog's different barks and their meanings. For example, the bark when someone comes to the door will be different than the bark when he is excited to see you. It is similar to a person's tone of voice, except that the dog has to rely totally on tone of voice because he does not have the benefit of using words—thank heavens! An incessant barker will be evident at an early age.

There are some things that encourage a dog to bark. For example, if your dog barks non-stop for a few minutes and you give him a treat to quiet him, he believes that you are rewarding him for barking. He will associate barking with getting a treat, and will keep doing it until he is rewarded.

FOOD STEALING

Is your dog devising ways of stealing food from your coffee table? If so, you must answer the following questions: Is your Cavalier hungry, or is he "constantly famished" like many dogs seem to be? Face it, some dogs are more food-motivated than others. Some dogs are totally obsessed by the smell of food and can only think of their next meal. Food stealing is terrific fun and always yields a great reward—FOOD, glorious food.

The owner's goal, therefore, is to be sensible about where food is placed in the home, and to reprimand your dog whenever caught in the act of stealing. But remember, only reprimand the dog if you

HE'S PROTECTING YOU

Barking is your dog's way of protecting you. If he barks at a stranger walking past your house, a moving car or a fleeing cat, he is merely exercising his responsibility to protect his pack (YOU) and territory from a perceived intruder. Since the "intruder" usually keeps going, the dog thinks his barking chased it away and he feels fulfilled. This behavior leads your overly vocal friend to believe that he is the "dog in charge."

THE ORIGIN OF THE DINNER BELL

The study of animal behavior can be traced back to the 1800s and the renowned psychologist, Pavlov. When it was time for his dogs to eat, Pavlov would ring a bell, then feed the dogs. Pavlov soon discovered that the dogs learned to associate the bell with food and would drool at the sound of a bell. And you thought yours was the only dog obsessed with eating!

actually see him stealing, not later when the crime is discovered for that will be of no use at all and will only serve to confuse.

BEGGING

Just like food stealing, begging is a favorite pastime of hungry puppies! It yields that same super reward—FOOD! Dogs quickly learn that their owners keep the "good food" for ourselves, and that we humans do not dine on dry food alone. Begging is a conditioned response related to a specific stimulus, time and place. The sounds of the kitchen, cans and bottles opening, crinkling bags, the smell of food in preparation, etc., will excite the dog and soon the paws are in the air!

Here is the solution to stopping this behavior: Never give in to a beggar! You are rewarding the dog for sitting pretty, jumping up, whining and rubbing his nose into you by giving him that glorious reward—food. By ignoring the dog, you will (eventually) force the behavior into extinction. Note that the behavior likely gets worse before it disappears, so be sure

Left to his own devices, even the youngest Cav puppy can find mischief between his incisors. Give your dog safe chew toys so that he can soothe his growing mouth.

there are not any "softies" in the family who will give in to little "Oliver" every time he whimpers, "More, please."

SEPARATION ANXIETY

Your Cavalier may howl, whine or otherwise vocalize his displeasure at your leaving the house and his being left alone. This is a normal reaction, no different than the child who cries as his mother leaves him on the first day at school. In fact, constant attention can lead to separation anxiety in the first place. If you are endlessly fussing over your dog, he will come to expect this from you all of the time and it will be more traumatic for him when you are not there. Obviously, you enjoy spending time with your dog, and he thrives on your love and attention. However, it should not become a dependent relationship where he is heartbroken without you.

One thing you can do to minimize separation anxiety is to make your entrances and exits as low-key as possible. Do not give your dog a long drawn-out goodbye, and do not lavish him with hugs and kisses when you return. This is giving in to the attention that he craves, and it will only make him miss it more when you are away. Another thing you can try is to give your dog a treat when you leave; this will not only keep him occupied and keep his mind off the fact that you have

just left, but it will also help him to associate your leaving with a pleasant experience.

You may have to accustom your dog to being left alone in intervals. Of course, when your dog

---

PHARMACEUTICAL FIX

There are two drugs specifically designed to treat mental problems in dogs. About seven million dogs each year are destroyed because owners can no longer tolerate their dogs' behavior, according to Nicholas Dodman, a specialist in animal behavior at Tufts University in Massachusetts.

The first drug, Clomicalm, is prescribed for dogs suffering from separation anxiety, which is said to cause them to react when left alone by barking, chewing their owners' belongings, drooling copiously or defecating or urinating inside the home.

The second drug, Anipryl, is recommended for cognitive dysfunction syndrome or "old-dog syndrome," a mental deterioration that comes with age. Such dogs often seem to forget that they were housebroken and where their food bowls are, and they may even fail to recognize their owners.

A tremendous human-animal bonding relationship is established with all dogs, particularly senior dogs. This precious relationship deteriorates when the dog does not recognize his master. The drug can restore the bond and make senior dogs feel more like their "old selves."

starts whimpering as you approach the door, your first instinct will be to run to him and comfort him, but do not do it! Eventually he will adjust and be just fine if you take it in small steps. His anxiety stems from being placed in an unfamiliar situation; by familiarizing him with being alone he will learn that he is okay. That is not to say you should purposely leave your dog home alone for long periods, but the dog needs to know that, while he can depend on you for his care, you do not have to be by his side 24 hours a day.

When the dog is alone in the house, he should be confined to his crate or designated dog-proof area of the house. This should be where he sleeps and already feels comfortable so he will feel more at ease when he is alone.

COPROPHAGIA

Feces eating is, to most humans, one of the most disgusting behaviors that their dog could engage in, yet to the dog it is perfectly normal. It is hard for us to understand why a dog would want to eat his own feces. He could be seeking certain nutrients that are missing from his diet; he could be just plain hungry; or he could be attracted by the pleasing (to a dog) scent. While coprophagia most often refers to the dog eating his own feces, a dog may just as likely eat that of another animal as well if he comes across it. Dogs often find the stool of cats and horses more palatable than that of other dogs. Vets have found that diets with a low digestibility, containing relatively low levels of fiber and high levels of starch, increase coprophagia. Therefore, high-fiber diets may decrease the likelihood of dogs' eating feces. Both the consistency of the stool (how firm it feels in the dog's mouth) and the presence of undigested nutrients increase the likelihood. Once the dog develops diarrhea from feces eating, he will likely quit this distasteful habit.

Reprimanding for stool eating rarely impresses the dog. Vets recommend distracting the dog while he is in the act of stool eating. Coprophagia is seen most frequently in pups 6 to 12 months of age, and usually disappears around the dog's first birthday.

To discourage this behavior, first make sure that the food you are feeding your dog is nutritionally complete and that he is getting enough food. If changes in his diet do not seem to work, and no medical cause can be found, you will have to modify the behavior before it becomes a daily habit through environmental control. The best way to prevent your dog from coprophagia is to make feces unavailable—clean up after he eliminates, remove any stool from the yard and keep your cat's litter boxes clean. If it is not there, he cannot eat it.

INDEX

My Cavalier King Charles Spaniel

PUT YOUR PUPPY'S FIRST PICTURE HERE

Dog's Name _____

Date _____ Photographer _____